Dare to Dream

DESIGN THE RETIREMENT
YOU CAN'T WAIT TO WAKE UP TO

Bryan J. Sweet, CLU®, ChFC®, MSFS, CFS
Sweet Financial Services

The information contained in this book does not purport to be a complete description of the securities, markets, or developments referred to in this material. The information has been obtained from sources considered to be reliable, but we do not guarantee that the material is accurate or complete. Any information is not a complete summary or statement of all available data necessary for making an investment decision and does not constitute a recommendation. Any opinions of the chapter authors are those of the chapter authors and not necessarily those of RJFS or Raymond James. Expressions of opinion are as of the initial book publishing date and are subject to change without notice.

Raymond James Financial Services, Inc., is not responsible for the consequences of any particular transaction or investment decision based on the content of this book. All financial, retirement, and estate planning should be individualized, as each person's situation is unique.

This information is not intended as a solicitation or an offer to buy or sell any security referred to herein. Keep in mind that there is no assurance that our recommendations or strategies will ultimately be successful or profitable or protect against a loss. There may also be the potential for missed growth opportunities that may occur after the sale of an investment. Recommendations, specific investments, or strategies discussed may not be suitable for all investors. Past performance may not be indicative of future results. You should discuss any tax or legal matters with the appropriate professional.

Investing involves risk, and you may incur a profit or loss, regardless of the strategy selected. Diversification does not ensure a profit or guarantee against a loss. The S&P 500 is an unmanaged index of 500 widely held stocks that is generally considered representative of the US stock market. The Dow Jones Industrial Average (DJIA), commonly known as "The Dow," is an index representing 30 stocks of companies maintained and reviewed by the editors of The Wall Street Journal.

Keep in mind that individuals cannot invest directly in any index, and index performance does not include transaction costs or other fees, which will affect actual investment performance. Individual investors' results will vary. Hypothetical examples in this book are for illustration purposes only and do not represent actual investments.

© 2016 by Sweet Financial Services. All rights reserved.
ISBN 13: 978-1539983453
ISBN 10: 1539983455

What People Are Saying About Dare to Dream

"A practical guide for retiring with an actual plan for all that matters most to you. Use this book as a creative, simple, and effective recipe for managing your money, your life' and your passion for a sparkling retirement."

Ed Slott
CPA and Retirement Expert
Founder of www.irahelp.com

"If retirement is part of your bigger future, the scorecards in this book will help open your eyes to a clear, actionable path from where you are to where you want to be. Bryan's years of accumulated wisdom in guiding people through both the math and the mindsets required to help achieve their retirement dreams are evident throughout."

Dan Sullivan
Founder
The Strategic Coach, Inc.

"After many years successfully assisting clients with preparing for and enjoying their retirement years, in this outstanding book Bryan provides a blueprint for getting the most out of life after stepping aside from running a business, working in a corporate environment, or teaching or caring for others. Readers will appreciate the straightforward, easy to understand and actionable recommendations to increase assets, financial and non-monetary, during retirement. And rather than read it once and put it on the bookshelf, this should become a reference manual and how to guide for anyone, or any couple, considering retirement. Highly recommended."

Scott A. Curtis
President
Raymond James Financial Services

"Bryan Sweet is the consummate professional in the financial services industry. He lives to serve his clients and devotes so much of his time to creating a client experience that is second to none. Bryan stays on the cutting edge from an investment and financial planning perspective by consistently attending seminars, lectures, study-group meetings, and coaching seminars. He has an enormous amount of knowledge and experience and thus has much to share."

Peter D. Maller, MBA, CFP®, AEP®
Founder and President
Maller Wealth Advisors
Lincoln Financial Network Advisor of the Year

"Bryan did it! He's condensed 30+ years of front line experience into a very readable book about achieving a better, more fulfilling retirement. Read it and start the adventure!"

James "Jim" B. Kruzan, CFP®, CRPC®
President
Kaydan Wealth Management

Dedication

Mary Beth—My partner in this amazing adventure since 1985. Your support has always been there, and never once over the years did I ever hear you talk or complain about the long hours, weekends, and evenings. I couldn't create amazing results without that special partner. So glad you've been with me on this journey. I love you.

Mom—I couldn't have asked for a more supportive childhood than I got from you. You set the standard in our one-parent household for how to become a good person and care about others. For that I will always be indebted. Love you.

Dick Ford—My first mentor. He showed me the ropes of how to be a professional, including how to tie a double Windsor knot for my necktie. His guidance, wisdom, and ultimately family friendship continue today. Unfortunately, God needed him more, and Dick left us too soon. We will always miss you. Thanks, Dick.

Roy and Jean Yeager—My aunt and uncle who have been with me since the beginning. Your insight and guidance on all things worldly helped shape my growth as a person. Your always-positive and supportive spirits are qualities you have transferred to me today.

Contents

Acknowledgments

Everything we do at Sweet Financial Services is a team effort focused on tailoring retirement solutions for our clients. Although my name is on the cover of this book, it has been a team effort as well. This book represents my close collaboration with Brittany Anderson, Director of Operations, and Oliver Kollofski, CFP®, CPWA®, Director of Wealth Services.

Because our entire team works closely together to design retirement solutions for our clients, the content of this book would not be possible without them. I value and appreciate all of the expertise, education, insight, professionalism, and passion the Sweet Financial Services team contributes to our firm and to our clients.

CHAPTER 1
The Costly Retirement
Mistakes People Make

"Success without fulfillment is the
ultimate failure."

—Tony Robbins
Motivational Speaker and Author

The statistics are discouraging—too few Americans are saving money for retirement. According to a 2016 GoBankingRates survey, one-third of Americans report they have no retirement savings. And 23 percent have saved less than $10,000. This means 56 percent of Americans have less than $10,000 saved for retirement.[1]

One definition of the word "retire" is to put something out of service. We think it's unfortunate that this potentially rewarding, blissful phase of life is attached to the word "retirement." The term just doesn't capture the joy, adventure, and fulfillment that await you after you leave your primary career. But because that is the commonly accepted term, we are using it.

Retirement is not a finish line; it's a starting point to what can be, with some planning, the most fulfilling years of your life. Too often, we see people just accept what happens to them after they leave the workforce rather than defining their dreams, planning for the future, and making it all happen the way they want.

Our Financial Situations Are More Complex than Ever

Most people have no idea what they need to do to prepare for retirement. As our lives and financial situations become more complex, planning for retirement can become increasingly overwhelming. This isn't surprising because no one teaches retirement planning in high school, college, or anywhere else. And in most cases, our parents weren't sure how to plan for retirement, either. Many of them simply relied on their pensions, which are now practically obsolete.

If you don't know what questions to ask yourself and how to prepare, you likely will reach retirement without a plan. People don't know what they don't know, so they often make poor decisions based on what they think is right, what a friend or neighbor did, or what they see on TV or read on the Internet.

As financial investments become more complex and consumers are inundated with more and more readily available (but not necessarily helpful) information, the need for a competent, compassionate financial advisor becomes increasingly critical. Even the most devoted do-it-yourselfers may find it extremely difficult to navigate all the complex aspects of financial and retirement planning and the constant changes in regulations, tax rates, and other details

> Even the most devoted do-it-yourselfers may find it extremely difficult to navigate all the complex aspects of financial and retirement planning.

---

1. Elyssa Kirkham, March 14, 2016, Money website, http://time.com/money/4258451/retirement-savings-survey/.

governing investments. Without the proper licensing, years of training, and hands-on experience in retirement planning, it is difficult to excel at tasks like retirement-account rebalancing, document management and archiving, compliance monitoring, data aggregation, portfolio administration, and research and analytics.

But even if you could do a great job at keeping up with the many details involved in designing an optimum retirement plan, do you really have the time for it? Wouldn't you rather spend your time making use of your unique talents?

Bill Schiffman, president and cofounder of Schiffman Grow & Co., describes his professional retirement-planning service for clients by saying, "I cut their financial lawns." He says, "I can cut my own grass. I choose not to because I feel like my time is better spent doing other things. I would stack my clients' intelligence against anyone else's in the business. All of my clients could ultimately manage their own money or do their own taxes. They choose not to. They maximize the value of their time by allowing me to do these things for them."[2]

Our goal is to use our retirement-planning expertise to provide you with an easy-to-follow road map for your financial success in a world of immense complexity and constant change.

The Costly Retirement Mistakes People Make Are Avoidable

We see many people make costly—and entirely avoidable—mistakes as they approach retirement. We specialize in helping people avoid these mistakes. In this book, you will learn how to avoid common retirement mistakes like these "tricky 10" that people make every day:

1. **Focusing only on the numbers instead of on what would make retirement fulfilling for them**

2. **Chasing returns on investments that aren't related to their goals.** For example, a neighbor will tell our client, "You should invest in this stock and get this return." But it's not related to the client's goals, so she ends up taking a lot more risk than she should. And then, when the market goes down a lot, either she overreacts and sells everything, or she does exactly the opposite and buys twice as much of that stock. We instruct people to focus on what's important to them. Rather than measuring yourself against an external index such as the S&P 500, we recommend that you create your own

2. Bill Crager and Jay Hummel, *The Essential Advisor: Building Value in the Investor–Advisor Relationship* (Hoboken, New Jersey: John Wiley & Sons, 2016), 32.

index, which is the rate of return needed to achieve your own personal goals.

3. **Making decisions alone instead of collaborating with their spouse.** It's important to acknowledge that although you and your spouse share many aspects of life, you each have unique dreams and aspirations. We encourage couples to acknowledge and pursue their own personal dreams while collaborating with one another to achieve their collective goals.

4. **Being so focused on the day-to-day activities of life and of running a business that they never stop to think about, or discuss, what the future should look like.** So often, people are so busy running on life's treadmill, they don't realize that perhaps they can make more progress by slowing down and focusing on specific goals and the strategies needed to reach them.

5. **Paying too much tax on their assets**

6. **Owning investments that don't match their true objectives**

7. **Focusing only on *accumulation* of wealth and not planning for the optimum *distribution* of wealth in retirement** (This topic is so important that we have devoted Chapter 4 to it.)

8. **Taking Social Security as soon as it's available without doing an analysis of their situation first**

9. **Having a negative "I can't do that" mind-set**

10. **Basing financial decisions on emotion instead of logic and planning**

One of the priceless benefits of having the right financial advisor is that he or she can help you avoid these common and costly mistakes.

One of the priceless benefits of having the right financial advisor—a Dream Architect (we describe the Dream Architect later in this chapter)—to act as your personal advocate and retirement-planning partner is that he or she can help you avoid these common and costly mistakes. We encourage you to work with an advisor who will tailor a retirement plan that aligns perfectly with the future you envision for yourself and your family.

Questions to Ask Yourself as You Assess Your Situation

You can avoid some of these mistakes by knowing where you stand in terms of planning for the future.

Here are some important questions you need to ask yourself about your own retirement. If you don't know how to answer them, it's OK. By the time you finish reading this book, you will have a clearer picture about what your retirement will look like and how you will get there.

1. What have you done to plan for the next 30 years of unemployment?

2. The IRS, your family, or charity will inherit your wealth, and you get to pick two of those three. Which ones have you chosen?

3. Do you have a triple-tax-free account?

4. Does it feel like you are getting double-taxed? That just might be the case.

5. Is your rate of return too high? No, that's not a misprint—it could actually be a problem!

6. Are you in what we call the "sweet spot" for tax planning? That is the time period between age 59.5 and age 70.5. It's the 11-year window of time in which the IRS allows, but doesn't require, penalty-free distributions from an IRA or 401(k) plan.

7. Is it possible that a college savings plan for either your children or grandchildren could be integrated with your retirement plan? A better option might be a plan that still benefits you if your plans to save for college change.

8. Have you evaluated any potential impact on your overall retirement

income plan since Social Security laws changed in May 2016?

9. Will your life insurance run out before you do? Do you *have* life insurance?

10. If something were to happen to you, do your loved ones know where to find all of your important documents?

11. Back in 2008 and 2009, did it feel like your 401(k) turned into a 201(k) because you lost so much money? Is it because you don't know your *risk* level?

12. Have you evaluated the health of your wealth?

13. If you have met with a financial advisor and received advice you weren't sure about, have you gotten a second opinion?

Retirement Concerns Keep Many People Awake at Night

In the days gone by, people had employer-guaranteed pensions from their long, stable tenure at their jobs. They sat back in retirement and collected those pensions, worry-free.

YOYO

"You're On Your Own" when it comes to retirement savings.

Those days are long gone. Financial services industry consultant Nick Murray sums this reality up with the acronym YOYO. It means "You're on your own!" The bottom line is that in today's world, you are responsible for accumulating your own retirement savings, whether through a 401(k) account, stocks, or other investments.

This fact keeps people up at night.

A survey by Ramsey Solutions said 56 percent of Americans are losing sleep over retirement. That includes both those who are saving and those who aren't. The survey reveals that Americans who work with a financial advisor are nearly twice as likely as those who do not to say they are "very confident" that they will have enough money to retire. Still another survey, from Schwab Retirement Plan Services, reports that saving enough for retirement is the top source of financial stress, even for millennials.[3]

According to a 2016 study by the T. Rowe Price group, college has become so expensive that even the parents of third-graders fear that college expenses will leave them too debt-saddled to retire. The study revealed that about three-quarters of parents of children ages 8 to 14 were willing to postpone

3. Rodney Brooks, "Saving for Retirement Brings Stress," *The Washington Post*, August 16, 2016.

retirement to pay for their children's college costs. About 68 percent of parents said they would be willing to get a second job to pay for college. Also, 42 percent of parents said they are losing sleep worrying about future college costs.[4]

People Often Underestimate the Costs of Medical Care in Retirement

It is difficult to project how much money a person will need for health care in retirement because no one knows how good or poor their health will be. But a 2016 report by Fidelity estimated that the average 65-year-old couple retiring in 2016 will need $260,000 to cover their medical expenses throughout retirement. And that number doesn't include the cost of long-term-care insurance, which can add another $130,000.[5]

Health care costs are rising steadily. In fact, they have grown at an annualized rate of 6 percent for the past 50 years. This means that today's health care costs are more than 18 times higher than they were in 1966.[6]

Not surprisingly, many Americans also lose sleep worrying about medical and long-term care costs in retirement. According to a 2014 survey by Allianz, about 67 percent of Americans ages 55 to 65 say medical expenses were the top retirement concern. Medical expenses and health care are the most misunderstood and underestimated expense for retirees. Consider these facts from retirement-planning expert Bob Carlson, who writes a newsletter called *Retirement Watch*:[7]

- Medicare pays only 80 percent of covered expenses, so you're on the hook for 20 percent with no limit. Plus, there are many medical expenses that Medicare doesn't cover.

---

4. Shahien Nasiripour, "The High Price of an Education," *Bloomberg News*, August 16, 2016.
5. "Retiree Health Costs Rise," August 16, 2016, Fidelity Investments website, https://www.fidelity.com/viewpoints/retirement/retiree-health-costs-rise.
6. Matthew Frankel, "Here's What the Typical American Retiree Spends on Health Care," October 17, 2016, *USA TODAY* website, http://www.usatoday.com/story/money/personalfinance/2016/10/17/health-care-cost-retiree-social-security/91887122/.
7. Bob Carlson, "The New Rules of Retirement," e-mail newsletter, August 23, 2016. You can read more about Bob at https://www.retirementwatch.com/about-bob-carlson/.

- Medicare covers only about half of the average member's medical expenses. The average retiree will pay $6,000 to $8,000 out-of-pocket each year for medical care. That's the average, so many pay more, and some pay considerably more.

- A retired married couple today is estimated to need, on average, more than $270,000 over the next 20 years to pay for their medical expenses that aren't covered by Medicare. Of course, those with above-average needs or who live past age 85 will need even more.

- Long-term care expenses generally aren't covered by Medicare. The truth is, Medicare pays for only a minority of nursing home expenses, and those payments largely are for short-term rehabilitation after an illness or injury. Residents and their families pay most nursing home expenses.

- Prescription drugs aren't covered by basic Medicare Parts A and B.

- Medicare is now means-tested. This means that the higher your income is, the higher your Medicare premiums will be for both regular Medicare Part B and for prescription drug coverage under Part D.

- The Affordable Care Act shifts money away from Medicare, especially the popular Medicare Advantage program, thus reducing benefits and increasing costs for beneficiaries.[8]

Being prepared for the medical costs alone is a huge reason to start planning for retirement as soon as possible.

The Solution: Work with a Dream Architect

Designing a retirement you can't wait to wake up to can be compared to the process of designing your dream home. It begins with a dream and a vision. It requires thoughtful planning, disciplined saving, and steady progress toward making it all happen in a specific time frame. We call financial advisors who understand this process "Dream Architects."

A Dream Architect is a competent, compassionate, financial advisor who is experienced in retirement planning and cares about your dreams and goals, not just about the amount of money you need to save. He or she can relieve the stress, remove the worry, and drastically decrease your likelihood of making mistakes related to your retirement.

If you already have a financial advisor, we encourage you to examine that

---

8. Ibid.

relationship to see if you are getting the optimum value for your money and effort. Often people stay with their financial advisor for years, even though he or she is not following up with them about their progress toward retirement or about changes in their financial situation resulting from major life events.

It's like staying with the same car insurance company for 25 years because it's easier than shopping around for a new one. It doesn't take any work if it's already set up, and it's comfortable to stay with what you know. But if you were to shop around, you might find that there were additional services you could have been taking advantage of for years.

If your advisor is indeed doing everything he or she should for you, that's great! But if not, then get a second opinion and find a Dream Architect who will encourage you to dream big and help you design the best retirement possible. While you're shopping, refer to Chapter 3 of this book. Review the nine qualities that characterize a Dream Architect and fill out our checklist of Dream Architect qualities for each advisor you visit so that you can compare them.

Whatever concerns, fears, anxieties, or questions you have about retirement, we have encountered them many times and have designed customized solutions for every client who has ever faced them. The information in this book will help demystify and simplify the topic of retirement planning for you.

You do not have to navigate the overwhelming process of retirement planning alone. We want to help you design a retirement that becomes the most fulfilling, exciting journey you have ever begun. Our dream for this book is to show you how easy, fun, and exciting it can be to plan the retirement that you can't wait to wake up to.

Chapter 1 Summary

Next Steps to Your Dream Retirement

Here are key steps discussed in this chapter that will start you on the path to designing the retirement you can't wait to wake up to:

1. Be aware of, and avoid, these common and costly retirement mistakes, the "tricky 10":

    -   Focusing only on the numbers instead of on what would make retirement fulfilling for you

    -   Chasing returns on investments that aren't related to your goals

    -   Making decisions alone instead of collaborating with your spouse

    -   Being so focused on the day-to-day activities of life and of running a business that you never stop to think about, or discuss, what the future should look like

    -   Paying too much tax on your assets

    -   Owning investments that don't match your true objectives

    -   Focusing only on accumulation of wealth and not planning for the optimum distribution of wealth in retirement

    -   Taking Social Security as soon as it's available without doing an analysis of your situation first

    -   Having a negative "I can't do that" mind-set

    -   Basing financial decisions on emotion instead of logic and planning

2. If you already work with a financial advisor, get a second opinion. Interview advisors who specialize in retirement planning so you can get the most out of your relationship with the person you choose.

3. Make a list of what keeps you up at night. Share it with your advisor, and discuss solutions.

CHAPTER 2
An Actionable Retirement: Living Your Why

"The tragedy in life doesn't lie in not reaching your goal. The tragedy lies in having no goal to reach."

—Benjamin E. Mays
American Minister, Activist, and Humanitarian

Few people know what their lives will look like after their primary careers have ended. In many cases, it's because they've been so busy accumulating wealth and taking care of day-to-day living that they have never sat down to figure out what types of activities they want to fill their time with after they leave the workforce.

And sadly, many people do not know *why* they are building wealth, beyond basic survival. They have not discovered the personal *why* that drives everything they do.

Put Your *Why* Before Your *What* and *How*

Simon Sinek is the author of the wildly successful book *Start with Why: How Great Leaders Inspire Everyone to Take Action*. He also delivered the third most-watched talk of all time on this topic on TED.com. Sinek defines your *why* simply as "The purpose, cause, or belief that inspires you to do what you do."[9]

Sinek says most people talk about *what* they do and then *how* they do it and finally *why* they do it. The ideal way to approach life is just the opposite—focusing on *why* you want to do something and then addressing *what* and *how*.

Your optimum retirement must be shaped around your personal *why*.

People often think about saving for retirement as a matter of willpower—having the ability to say no to something they want so they can save more for the future. But forget about willpower! Focus instead on "why" power. The wisest and most motivating choices are the ones that align with what you identify as your purpose, your core self, and your highest values. Your choices in life are meaningful only when you connect them to your desires and dreams.

In this book, we discuss dreams a lot. Here is our definition of a dream:

> A dream is a pleasurable vision of what the future can become that fills you with energy, speaks to your heart, and strengthens your will and ability to overcome all roadblocks to achieve it.

In Chapter 6, we introduce you to a tool we use to help our clients discover their personal *why*. It's called the Dream Architect process, and it enables you to learn more about what motivates you.

---

9. Simon Sinek, "Start with Why" website, https://www.startwithwhy.com/About.aspx.

Your Personal Why Defines Your Mind-Set

Retirement is much more than the numbers; it's both math and mind-set.

The financial part is easy. For example, if you say you will need $5,000 a month in retirement, once you are no longer receiving a paycheck, then in less than an hour, we can probably tell you how much money you need to have saved by the time you retire.

But that is way too basic. What are you going to do with that $5,000? What types of life experiences do you want to have over the years, and how can we help make them happen? Without asking yourself these types of questions, you're setting yourself up for a potentially dull and boring retirement. We ask questions that allow us to get a more in-depth view of what you want to *accomplish* in retirement. So if you say you want to have a summer home on Cape Cod, we will ask you, "*Why* is that important to you?" We will ask you "Why?" again and again until we get to the burning "why" deep down inside you that motivates you to wake up every morning.

If you answer the question from many different angles, it will shed light on your personal *why*, which, again, is the most important factor driving your retirement goals. Some of our clients actually shed tears when we begin to dig deep to find out the reason they are trying to accomplish something. In most cases, no one has ever asked them that question—"Why do you want that particular thing when you retire?" We have found that if something has deep personal meaning to you, you will be more likely to make the changes necessary in your habits and lifestyle to achieve that goal.

Because every client has unique goals and dreams, the questions we ask are different for every single person we meet with.

Retire by Design, Not by Happenstance

Imagine that you are searching for a home that is just right for you and your family. Your real estate agent knows what you are looking for and shows you a lot of different homes in various neighborhoods. But you cannot find one home that has all the features you want. It can be frustrating. You might like the kitchen in one house, but the bedrooms are too small. In another home, you might like the in-law suite, but there is no fireplace. You end up compromising—getting some things you want but doing without others that are just as important to you.

Now imagine that you design your own home with every feature and amenity you've always wanted. You can plan your home from the ground up and not compromise! You will get every single item on your wish list. That's what it's like when you design the retirement you can't wait to wake up to.

That is the purpose of working with a Dream Architect—a competent, compassionate advisor who will work with you to design your ideal retirement so that you can check every single item off your bucket list. This type of planning will give you control of the outcome because you will have input about what happens during every step of the process. When you plan your retirement, you will know what you want and what it will take to get there. You are *designing* your dreams, not just waiting to see what happens when you retire and hoping for the best.

> A well-designed retirement plan that is tailored to your situation and your dreams for the future will help guide you through every step of the process.

Retirement planning is like using GPS technology to find an address when you're driving in an unfamiliar place. Your GPS device will tell you exactly when and where to turn. Without it, you would be driving in circles, lost. A well-designed retirement plan that is tailored to your situation and your dreams for the future will help guide you through every step of the process. You will arrive at your destination on time, feeling confident and relaxed.

Failing to Plan Can Lead to Disaster

No matter how much you think you've planned and no matter how wealthy you are, without proper planning and without a Dream Architect guiding you, statistics say that one in five people can go broke. A 2015 analysis by the Employee Benefits Research Institute found that of those people 85 or older who died between 2010 and 2012, roughly one in five had no assets other than a house, and the average home equity was about $140,000. Roughly one in eight of those households had no assets at all.[10] It is important to find and work with a Dream Architect who has comprehensive planning capabilities

---

10. John W. Schoen, "Among Oldest Americans, One in Five Dies Broke," CNBC website, http://www.cnbc.com/2015/04/29/among-oldest-americans-1-in-5-dies-broke.html.

to enable you to enter retirement confidently.

Unfortunately, a lot of people get to retirement and at age 62, 65, or 67 and make some assumptions about the size of nest egg they'll need in retirement, based on what they've heard. But they don't do an in-depth analysis to find out what their lives will look like in retirement and what they are trying to accomplish.

You can't afford to make bad decisions in retirement. If you are nearing retirement age, you don't have time to correct financial mistakes. Too many people end up having to go back to work because they didn't analyze their situation before retiring.

Also, too many people think they can rely only on Social Security when they retire. Unfortunately, that is a myth.

Another risk many people face in retirement is failing to define their personal identities outside of their work and professions. In their book *Your Retirement Quest*, Keith Lawrence and Alan Spector note that the highest suicide rate in our country today is among men over the age of 70, who struggle to replace the purpose they found at work once they are no longer working. And the fastest-growing divorce rate is among couples over the age of 55, as relationship issues are heightened once partners are together much more during retirement.

Planning can help you avoid these common and horrific consequences of not being prepared for this very different phase of your life.

Of course there are some things we can't control, such as the 9/11 attacks in 2001 or the stock market crash of 2008. But there is a lot that we *can* control and plan for. We hope you will sit down with a competent and compassionate financial advisor who will analyze your specific situation, learn what your dreams are, and help you design a retirement plan that makes your future the best it can be.

Consider Working Longer

One way to be prepared for the possibility of not having enough money in retirement is to consider working longer than you might have anticipated.

In August 2016, TransAmerica released its 17th annual Retirement Survey of Workers, titled *Perspectives on Retirement: Baby Boomers, Generation X, Millennials*. The report noted that roughly two-thirds of Baby Boomers plan to work past age 65 (or already are working past that age). This is actually an incredibly positive sign, according to Jeffrey Levine, Director of Retirement Education for *The Slott Report*. He cites three reasons why working well into your 60s and beyond can be a big boost to your financial situation in retirement—in addition to the physical and mental health benefits so many studies have shown exist:

1. **First, working past 65 means that you'd generally be working until at least your full retirement age for Social Security benefit purposes.** Currently, full retirement age is 66, but for those born in 1955 and later, it gradually increases to 67. If you claim Social Security benefits prior to full retirement age, your benefit will be reduced. Of course, if you're still working, there's a much better chance that you won't need to claim your Social Security benefits prior to full retirement age.

   Not to mention that, thanks to the earnings limits imposed by Social Security prior to full retirement age, if your earnings are large enough, you wouldn't receive any Social Security benefits, even if you had already applied for them. At full retirement age, you could claim your Social Security benefits and continue working without fear of having your Social Security benefit reduced. That said, waiting to claim those benefits even longer could make sense, thanks to the 8 percent annual delayed credits you could receive, up until age 70.

2. **It gives you a good opportunity to continue to add to your nest egg.** By the time you reach your mid-60s, expenses have often dropped to a minimum. By that time, many have finished paying off the mortgage on their homes and/or college expenses for children. Turning 65 also typically means enrolling in Medicare, which can be a huge savings for some. Thus, at 65, 66, 67, and beyond, you may be able to sock away more in savings annually than you ever had before.

3. **Perhaps the biggest benefit of working well into your 60s is that it allows you to delay dipping into your nest egg longer.** The longer you hold off on doing that, the better you are. Investments can

continue to grow and compound. Perhaps most importantly, for each year you continue to work, the unknown amount of time you'll spend in retirement, draining your assets, will be reduced by one year. With medical advances continuing to extend life expectancies, this is hugely important.[11]

So don't consider working longer to be a bad thing. If you don't enjoy the work you've been doing, look for a second career that you can enjoy during retirement. It doesn't have to be drudgery. With some planning, it can be fun!

Believe Your Dreams Are Possible

Planning for retirement requires a positive "I can do that" attitude. Unfortunately, that kind of positive attitude can be off-putting to negative people. We see a lot of people who hear from their friends, acquaintances, and family members things like, "You can't do that" or "Oh, that's just wishful thinking." And then if you watch the news—CNN stands for "Chronically Negative News"—it compounds our society's chronically negative thinking because we are bombarded with stories and images of the worst imaginable scenarios in life.

Darren Hardy is the former publisher of *SUCCESS* magazine. In his best-selling book *The Compound Effect*, he compares a glass of dirty water to our minds when they become filled with negativity. Here is how Hardy explains this concept:

> What is influencing and directing your thoughts? The answer: whatever you're allowing yourself to hear and see. This is the input you are feeding your brain. Period.
>
> Your mind is like an empty glass; it'll hold anything you put into it. You put in sensational news, salacious headlines, talk-show rants, and you're pouring dirty water into your glass. If you've got dark, dismal, worrisome water in your glass, everything you create will be filtered through that muddy mess because that's what you'll be thinking about. Garbage in, garbage out.

11. Jeffrey Levine, "What TransAmerica Retirement Survey Says About Retirement Outlook," *The Slott Report*, September 14, 2016.

All that drive-time radio yak about murders, conspiracy, deaths, economy, and political battles drives your thinking process, which drives your expectations, which drives your creative output. That *is* bad news.

But just like a dirty glass, if you flush it with clean, clear water under the faucet long enough, eventually you'll end up with a glass of pure, clear water. What is that clear water? Positive, inspirational, and supportive input and ideas. Stories of aspiration—people who, despite challenges, are overcoming obstacles and achieving great things. Strategies of success, prosperity, health, love, and joy. Ideas to create more abundance, to grow, expand, and become more. Examples and stories of what's good, right, and possible in the world.[12]

So when you're constantly putting good energy, inspiration, and positive thinking into your life, over time it automatically filters out the bad and gets your mind in the right spot.

One way to fill your mind with positivity is to collect positive quotes and affirmations that mean something to you. Here are just a few of the beliefs we try to live by. They were written by Hal Elrod, author of *The Miracle Morning: The Not-So-Obvious Secret Guaranteed to Transform Your Life (Before 8:00 a.m.)*.

1. Anything is possible if you are committed.

2. Your level of success will rarely exceed your level of personal development because success is something you attract by the person you become.

3. If you want your life to be different, you have to be willing to do something different first.

4. One of the saddest things in life is to get to the end and look back in regret, knowing that you could have been, done, and had so much more.

5. Always remember that where you are is a result of who you were, but where you go depends entirely on who you choose to be from this moment on.

6. An extraordinary life is all about daily, continuous improvements in the areas that matter most.

12. Darren Hardy, *The Compound Effect* (New York: Vanguard Press, 2012), 121–2.

7. Whether you think you can, or you think you can't, you're right either way.

8. Your life gets better only after you get better.

9. The greatest gift we can give to the people we love is to live to our full potential.

10. If you don't make time for exercise, you'll probably have to make time for illness.

11. Do what's right, not what's easy.

12. Don't worry about trying to impress people. Just focus on how you can add value to their lives.

13. There is nothing to fear because you cannot fail. Just learn, grow, and become better than you've ever been before.

14. Who you're becoming is far more important than what you're doing. Yet it is what you're doing that is determining who you're becoming.

15. The average person lets *emotions* dictate his or her actions; achievers let their *commitments* dictate their actions.

16. Success looks easy to those who weren't there when the hard work was being done.

17. Everything new feels like a failure when you're in the middle of it.

A Personal Success Story About Positive Affirmation

I am a testament to the importance of having someone believe in you. Years ago, before our firm was at the level it is at now, the CEO of our broker dealer pulled me aside and said, "I see in you everything that would make you one of the most successful financial advisors in the company." I have never forgotten that. I finally had a clear vision of where I wanted to go and the confidence to get there. Because of that encouraging comment, we have taken specific actions to get to that level. Just like when you're planning for your retirement, we had to set specific measurable goals so that we would have a road map to follow and a clear target to aim for. I created the proper habits for my journey, so now we are among the top half of 1 percent of the advisors at my broker dealer.

Don't Give Up Until You Have Achieved Your Dreams

Thomas Edison said, "Many of life's failures are people who did not realize how close they were to success when they gave up." Too many people define their dreams and work on them for a while, but for various reasons, they get discouraged and give up.

Back in the gold-mining days, an ambitious miner prospected for gold for years and years but didn't find any. He finally gave up and sold his equipment to a man who enlisted the help of an engineer. That engineer discovered that the original miner had stopped drilling just three feet away from millions of dollars of ore! The miner had no idea how close he was to the biggest gold find in history. He simply gave up too early.

Much of the time, people don't realize how close they are to accomplishing their dreams. It helps a lot to have someone to help motivate you and keep you on track. If you have somebody cheering you on, it makes it a little bit easier to keep pushing forward when you don't want to keep going. That is what we do best.

We want to be the resource and the advocate to get people to stop the "stinkin' thinkin'." We want you to believe—to know—your dreams are possible.

If you want a better life, and if you have dreams and aspirations, stop listening to the people who have a "no" mentality. Focus on your own personal, unique dreams—your personal *why*. Hopefully we can be a resource to help you accomplish those dreams and truly live a better life—starting now and continuing through retirement.

You get only one shot at life. Why not make it the best one you can possibly have? Dare to dream!

Chapter 2 Summary

Next Steps to Your Dream Retirement

1. Determine and write down your retirement goals and your personal "why"—why those are your goals. Every financial decision you make as you prepare for retirement will center around your personal *why*.

2. If your retirement savings are not as ample as you would like, consider what you're passionate about. You will be amazed at the opportunities that present themselves when you pursue those passions. We have seen clients start a second career in their 60s and beyond, based on focusing on what fulfills them most.

3. Avoid negative people; surround yourself with people who support your goals and aspirations and encourage you.

4. Don't give up until you have achieved your dreams!

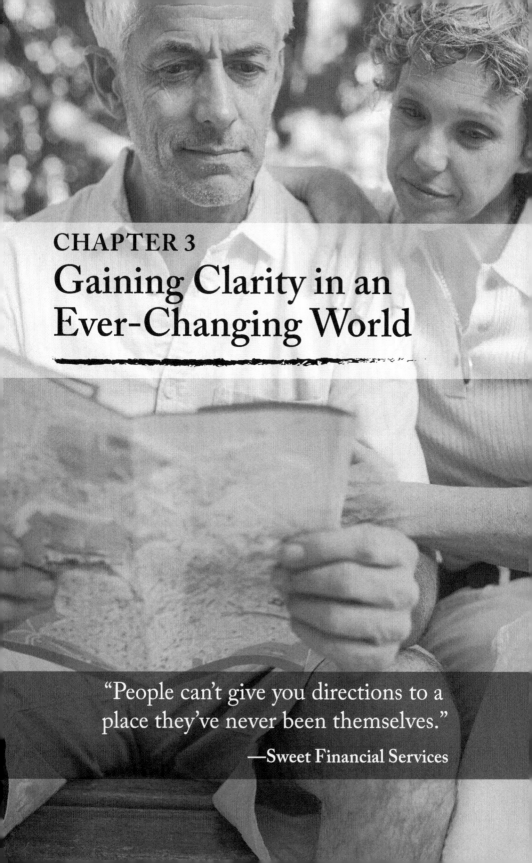

CHAPTER 3
Gaining Clarity in an Ever-Changing World

"People can't give you directions to a place they've never been themselves."

—Sweet Financial Services

To build an effective retirement plan, it's necessary to gain clarity about what you want your retirement to look like. A vague idea about what you want isn't enough. We are here to make the invisible visible to you and help put your future in focus.

One way we do that is by working with clients to set SMART goals—goals that are:

Specific
Measurable
Achievable
Realistic
Time-based

Having SMART goals written down increases your likelihood of success.

If you know what you want to accomplish, believe you can accomplish it, and know what successful people do to get there, you will be more likely to start doing the things successful people do. Success leaves a trail. You don't need to invent the process; you just need to repeat the habits that successful people have.

Being Clear About Your Goals Can Dissolve the Fear

Because retirement planning isn't well understood, we see a lot of fear surrounding it. Again, most of us learn nothing about planning for retirement when we're growing up, so it isn't surprising that few people understand how to go about it. Where there is a lack of understanding, there is fear. And where there is fear, there is avoidance. Most people avoid figuring out their goals, which is a mistake because goal setting is one of the best ways to dissolve the fear.

To gain clarity about what you really want in retirement, ask yourself a few questions. The more questions you ask yourself, the better your retirement plan will be. Here are a few important ones to get you started.

1. **What do you want to do for the rest of your life?** What does your ideal retirement look like? What are some things you would like to do that you have never had time for? Think beyond material possessions—think about *experiences* you've never had. One of our retired clients was in Rio de Janeiro recently, and he went

parasailing. He said he jumped off a perfectly good cliff while attached to a kite, and the experience was exhilarating for him. Life is about experiences. What experiences do you want to have that you can look back on with fond memories? What would make your life different and fulfilling? We have a great time guiding people to discover what those experiences might be.

2. **When was the last time you sat down and spent quality time discussing your collective goals with those closest to you—your spouse, family, and friends?** Think about how energized it made you feel. But how long ago did you have a discussion like that? Too long ago? Or maybe you have *never* discussed your goals with the people closest to you. We're not talking about a casual conversation before you rush off to the next activity. We're talking about an in-depth, open dialogue in which you discuss all sorts of ideas for the future—a conversation that really gets you motivated. If you have never done this, that's OK. Now is the time to start. And if you have discussed your goals with your loved ones, make sure you write down all the details and share this information with your Dream Architect.

3. **Do you have a defined plan that details what you want your money to do for you?** This goes way beyond everyday expenses such as food and utilities. So far beyond, in fact, that we're talking about the years while you're in retirement and even after you're gone. The possibilities are limitless—you have the opportunity to define what your future looks like. Again, if you haven't defined such a plan, that's OK. This book can help you get started.

4. **Is there a huge gap between your dreams and reality?** If there is, we have great news—you are not alone! This is a common issue we help clients with every day.

Here is just one example. We sat down with a couple recently to do some planning. All indications point to them having it all together, with a lot of assets, a successful manufacturing business, two grown children and wonderful grandchildren, and a winter home in the southeast. But when we asked them what they aspire to achieve over the next 5, 10, and 15+ years, they gave us blank stares, as if they didn't understand our question.

Then the wife said, "Every day, when my husband comes home from work, he is dejected and frustrated by things that happen at the business we own."

Our response was, "Wait a minute! This business is highly profitable, very professional, has a great reputation in the manufacturing industry, and produces cutting-edge, innovative products…but it's not fulfilling?"

> **We were able to help them focus more on the future and start getting excited about the kind of life they could live in retirement.**

The husband elaborated, saying he enjoys certain aspects of his current work, but the day-to-day aspects are so draining that they don't have time to think about tomorrow. We met with the couple, analyzed their situation, and asked them to describe their personal dreams and goals—and why they are important. After careful planning with them, we were able to help them focus more on the future and start getting excited about the kind of life they could live in retirement.

This seems to be more the rule rather than the exception. Most people tell us no one has ever asked them these questions before. To them, retirement has always been about the numbers. They have never allowed themselves to dream about their ideal retirement, so the concept is foreign to them at first. But once we start discussing their hopes and dreams, they realize that this is a much better way of looking at the whole process. They realize that they do want a better life, and they can begin to see that by setting goals and doing some planning, they can create the most fulfilling life possible. It is so rewarding when a client finally says, "*Why wouldn't I* want to go through that experience and build those dreams into my financial plan?"

5. **"What am I retiring from, and what am I retiring to?"** This is the *single most important question* you can ask yourself as you discover what your future should look like. Maybe you shouldn't retire yet. Or

at all. Or maybe you should be doing a different type of work than you're doing now. Would it be more fulfilling for you to do something rewarding that pays less than you earn now? We want you to get the most out of your retirement and fill your days with all the things you love. To accomplish that, again, you need to know what your personal *why* is. Maybe you are retiring from structured scheduling in the manufacturing business to a more relaxed schedule that includes spending time with your grandkids, developing your hobbies, and working part time in a job you're passionate about. Do you have a dream of living in New England, but you've never even visited there? Test it out! Do you want to take up a hobby like hiking, knitting, or painting, but you've never tried it? Test all of your dreams out to see if they live up to the way you are envisioning them.

Before you leave your company's parking lot for the last time, know what type of retirement will fulfill you—not just financially, but emotionally, mentally, and physically as well. What are you going to do with all that time you're going to have? What are you going to do after you read the newspaper each morning?

We believe that if you know what your personal *why* is and really set your mind to achieving your dreams, anything is possible. We see it happen every day—people achieving the exciting dreams they have planned for.

The Qualities of a Dream Architect

People can't give you directions to a place they've never been themselves. Often, people are influenced to make important financial decisions based on something they heard from a neighbor who hasn't retired yet or from an advisor who has never guided anyone through retirement. We want to reiterate how critical it is to find *a Dream Architect* to guide you through your retirement decisions.

As we mentioned in Chapter 1, a Dream Architect understands more than just the mathematical portion of the retirement-savings process—he or she is invested in discovering what your dreams and goals are for your retirement years. A Dream Architect specializes in helping to make retirement dreams come true.

Retirement planning is a transformational process. Many steps are involved, and your Dream Architect will understand your financial situation and your aspirations well as you go through the process of retirement planning together. Many financial advisors do business on a transactional basis—one transaction at a time. We believe a holistic, comprehensive retirement-planning process transforms people for the better.

We come across a lot of situations in which clients have worked with financial advisors who do not understand all the important aspects of retirement planning. For example, recently one of our clients brought in one of her mother's IRA account statements. She questioned whether the required minimum distribution that her mom was taking was correct. It was correct, but the advisor they were working with didn't know how it was calculated. He gave her the right answer only because it was printed on the statement from the brokerage company.

Many financial advisors today do little more than sell investments. A Dream Architect does much more than that. Here is a list of the qualities we think characterize a Dream Architect. He or she:

1. **Specializes in comprehensive wealth planning and practices advanced planning.** A comprehensive wealth planner offers retirement planning, asset preservation solutions, and investment services. He or she takes a holistic approach to your finances, paying attention to the fine details so that you are provided with the best advice possible. Not every advisor can provide these services.

    You deserve a holistic, big-picture approach to your finances. That's what you should be paying a financial advisor to do. And although it might seem like you would pay more for comprehensive financial advice than for investment planning, that is not always the case. We have had many clients tell us they get a lot more value from our comprehensive planning process than they have gotten from the basic investment advising they've received in the past.

    If you go to a repair shop because you need an oil change and new brakes, but the technician knows only how to change your oil, then you're getting only a portion of the service you need. It's the same with retirement planning—investments are only a small piece of the puzzle, but that is all some advisors do.

2. **Is knowledgeable about, and has experience in, designing retirement plans for clients.** A Dream Architect understands that in planning for retirement, there is a big difference between wealth *accumulation* and wealth *distribution*. Most people know the basics of wealth accumulation but do not understand the laws, rules, and strategies related to wealth *distribution* in retirement—in other words, taking money out of your accounts to live on.

3. **Recognizes the importance of the *mind-set* part of the equation, not just the *math* part.** In other words, the advisor understands that your retirement plan should be built around your unique set of hopes, dreams, and aspirations for the future. To start creating the retirement you can't wait to wake up to, go to sweetfinancial-1892961.hs-sites.com/dream-architect-assessment to take our team's Dream Architect Assessment, which will help you gain clarity on eight mind-sets we have found to be most important when working with a Dream Architect.

4. **Takes a team approach.** Working with a team as opposed to an individual advisor ensures a more thorough approach to the design of optimum solutions for your unique situation. It also ensures prompt attention to all of your concerns, even if the advisor you typically work with is out of the office, retires before you do, or dies. Choose an advisor who has a team of people who are professionals in their fields and have succession plans in place. It would be unfortunate to have your advisor retire or pass away, only to be turned over to a brand-new advisor whom you have never met and whom you would have to "train" on how to be your advisor. In a team environment, if something were to happen to your advisor, his or her team has already been part of all your planning and can continue to provide advice based on your goals.

5. **Understands the importance of working closely with your tax advisor, attorney, estate planner, and other professionals and does so without hesitation.** We work with clients' tax accountants daily because everyone pays taxes and needs guidance regarding the tax implications of the financial actions they take. And for clients who do not currently have a tax accountant, we recommend one. You would be amazed at the money-saving opportunities we find on tax returns.

> You would be amazed at the money-saving opportunities we find on tax returns.

For example, people don't know that they can convert their IRA to a Roth with little or no tax, just by being proactive. And unfortunately, most people wait until January or February to prepare their taxes, not realizing that there was an action they should have taken before December 31st of the previous year to get the optimum return. Consulting with your tax accountant is always key before making major changes to your investment allocations, especially in non-retirement accounts. What may be great in one area might be a disaster in another, so looking at the big picture is a must.

We also recommend attorneys to our clients who need guidance on wills, trusts, and complex estate-planning matters. Your advisor must help ensure that your retirement plan and strategies cover all necessary areas appropriately and thoroughly.

6. **Believes in continual growth and education.** For a wealth-planning firm to provide the best service possible to its clients, it is important for its team to have a culture that is focused on growth and education. It is through this practice that a firm can continue to grow and stay ahead of its clients' needs. What outside training is your advisor and his or her team taking on a continual basis to stay on the cutting edge? Some of the current programs we participate in continuously are Strategic Coach, Ed Slott's IRA/retirement coaching, Genius Network, and PEAK Advisor Alliance.

7. **Is proactive about assessing your situation on an ongoing basis.** A Dream Architect frequently handles complex items for you before they even come to your attention. He or she will keep an eye on your investments and life changes and constantly be looking for ways to take the guesswork out of the equation. One of the most common

complaints we hear from people is that their former financial advisor never called them for portfolio reviews. Make sure your advisor is doing this on a consistent basis. Ongoing review meetings each year are key to success.

8. **Is transparent and acts as your fiduciary.** He or she is fee-based to reduce conflicts of interest and always acts in your best interest. If unsure about this, ask your advisor if he or she is a fiduciary. Your advisor should be able to show you his or her ADV registration. (The ADV is the form that investment advisors use to register with both the Securities and Exchange Commission and state securities authorities.)

In 2016, the US Department of Labor issued a new ruling that requires anyone who provides retirement investment advice to abide by a "fiduciary" standard. In other words, they must put their clients' best interest before their own profits. Compliance is required as of April 10, 2017.[13]

It seems like a no-brainer, that everyone in this industry would work in your best interest. But most people in this business actually are

13. "Fact Sheet: Department of Labor Finalizes Rule to Address Conflicts of Interest in Retirement Advice, Saving Middle-Class Families Billions of Dollars Every Year," US Department of Labor, Employee Benefits Security Administration website, https://www.dol.gov/agencies/ebsa/about-ebsa/our-activities/resource-center/fact-sheets/dol-final-rule-to-address-conflicts-of-interest.

not fiduciaries, so there are built-in conflicts in their practices. The new Department of Labor ruling applies to IRAs and retirement accounts only, but we think it's just a matter of time before it applies to everything.

9. **Works closely with you for the long term.** Designing your retirement plan is just the first step; you and your advisor need to refer to it constantly to ensure that every financial decision you make is aligned with your personal goals. It is important for you to work with an advisor you feel comfortable calling to ask what he or she thinks about a big-ticket purchase. These are the types of decisions that can derail your plan. A Dream Architect will examine your situation to see if that's a wise move or not. If it's not, he or she will advise you about alternative solutions and tell you what needs to happen before you do make that purchase.

   A Dream Architect will keep an eye on your financial plan and recommend adjustments as necessary, based on major changes in your life, inflation, and market fluctuations. A Dream Architect is a *financial coach* who guides and supports your journey to and into retirement.

If you want to see if you are working with someone who can provide all of the solutions above—a Dream Architect—go to our website at http://www.sweetfinancial.com/services/second-opinion/ and take our Right Fit Advisor Assessment.

Or, if you prefer to use a simple list you can print out now, we have created a checklist to take with you when you visit financial advisors to get your second opinion. Print and complete the checklist on the next two pages when you visit each financial advisor. Then you can compare the advisors and decide whom you want to be your Dream Architect.

Checklist for Interviewing Dream Architects

		Yes	No

1. Comprehensive planning
Does this advisor specialize in comprehensive wealth planning and practice advanced planning? In other words, does he or she offer retirement planning, asset preservation solutions, and investment services rather than just investments? ☐ ☐

2. Retirement planning expertise
Does he or she have knowledge of and experience in designing retirement plans for clients? ☐ ☐

3. A focus on your dreams for the future
Does he or she recognize the importance of the *mind-set* part of the equation in addition to the *math* part? In other words, does this advisor understand that your retirement plan should be built around your unique set of hopes, dreams, and aspirations for the future? ☐ ☐

4. A team approach in his or her office
Does this advisor work with a team instead of alone to ensure that you receive advice from professionals in a lot of different areas of planning and to ensure that there is continuity if the advisor retires or dies? ☐ ☐

5. Coordination with your financial team
Does he or she understand the importance of working closely with your tax accountant, tax advisor, attorney, estate planner, and other professionals, and will he or she do so without hesitation? ☐ ☐

6. Lifelong learning
Does he or she believe in continual growth and education to keep up with changing regulations and to stay one step ahead of your needs? ☐ ☐

	Yes	No
7. **Proactive review of your situation** Will this advisor be proactive about keeping an eye on your investments and life changes and constantly be looking for ways to take the guesswork out of the equation for you?	❐	❐
8. **Transparency** Will this advisor be transparent and fee-based and act as your fiduciary?	❐	❐
9. **Long-term relationship** Will he or she work closely with you for the long term, through the accumulation phase of your retirement and into the distribution phase?	❐	❐

Number of Yes's for this advisor: _____
Number of No's for this advisor: _____

If you did not answer yes to all of these questions, it is a good idea to consider getting a second opinion about your retirement planning.

Dare to Dream

When you close your eyes and think about your first day of retirement, what do you see? Maybe you're sleeping until 10:00 a.m. Maybe you're taking Rover for the longest walk of his life. But what are you going to do the next day and the day after that? What about 10 years after that?

We can use the mind's eye to imagine what we want from life, now and down the road. Simply picture the possibilities:

- Think about what you're good at, what you enjoy doing, and what you've always wanted to try.

- Let your mind focus on those things, and begin to imagine yourself doing them at 60, 70, and 80.

- Pay attention to some of the larger aspects. Did your mind conjure an island scene? An office? Then imagine the smaller things that make up your daily life. Perhaps you're sitting with your friends at the country club. Or perhaps your grandkids are frolicking in your saltwater pool. Whatever passion pops into your head, share it with your spouse and the rest of your family so you can work toward this vision.

- It helps if you get into the habit of consistently "daydreaming" about the future, filling in details as they come to you and documenting them somewhere.

Now, what if you've paid all your bills and built a substantial cash cushion and find yourself pining over that classic automobile that needs just a little restoration? Seriously consider it! The amount of joy it brings can't be measured; just don't expect your prized possession to turn a profit as an investment.

When you're drifting off to sleep tonight, let your mind wander over the possibilities. Your bucket list is limited only by your imagination and your ability to plan and save to make your dreams come true.

Do a Practice Run

Before you retire, practice doing what you thought you would want to do in retirement in advance. You want to make sure it's actually something you want to do.

Many people work for most of their lives, often beginning when they are teenagers. After working for 50 years, it is really difficult to imagine anything different than driving to the office every day and putting in a full day of work. It's hard to even imagine what it would be like to wake up on a Monday morning and not have to drive to the office.

That might sound blissful, but when it actually happens, it turns out to be unfamiliar and uncomfortable for a lot of people. If they haven't planned their retirement in advance, they have no idea what to do all day.

To avoid surprises once you do retire, answer these questions now:

1. What will I do after reading the paper each morning?

2. What's on my bucket list?

3. How much traveling do we want to do? How often, and where?

4. What charitable organizations could use my skills as a volunteer?

5. How often would I volunteer?

6. What do I need to do to feel fulfilled?

Again, remember the most important question to ask yourself about your retirement: "What am I retiring from, and what am I retiring to?"

If you don't have it somewhat preplanned, it's going to be easy just to sit on the porch and rock in your rocker, or watch reruns of TV shows. Think about the things you truly love to do and the impact you want to leave. If you don't plan for them, they may not happen, or they may not happen the way that you want them to. Consider it a "practice run" for your retirement.

Plan It Like a Long-Term Vacation

Most people put more time and effort into planning their two-week vacations than they do planning for retirement. Think of your retirement as a 30-year vacation, and plan out all of the details:

1. How much money will you need, and what will you spend it on?

2. Which tours will you take?

3. Which fancy restaurants will you try?

4. Which organizations would you like to be involved with and serve on their boards?

5. What are your hobbies you haven't had the chance to pursue? Which hobbies do you have now that you want to pursue more?

6. What are some activities associated with those hobbies that you haven't done that you'd like to do?

7. Where will you learn about them? Do you need to take some classes or travel to go learn how to paraglide or build wooden canoes?

These are the types of questions your Dream Architect should be asking you. It takes a lot of digging deep to discover what you really love and want to do more of once you're not working every day.

> **It's important to define your vision for your retirement and work toward it.**

What we have found is that if you don't think about it, plan how you're going to do it, and then have somebody be accountable for it, which is part of our Dream Architect process, it can get away from you. It's easy let one day go into a week, and then into a month, and then a year, and you never accomplish anything. That's a pretty boring retirement.

That's why it's important to define your vision for your retirement and work toward it. It's also important to ensure that your vision is realistic and is really what you want. Consider the following two hypothetical examples in which one couple plans for something that they think they'd like but ends up being disappointed. A second couple defines their vision of the future based on what they know they enjoy.

36

Two Examples

The Duncans say their retirement dream is to retire in Florida because they have heard that a lot of people move to Florida to retire, so it seems like the thing to do. But they have never even been to Florida, and they don't know anyone there. That is not an ideal situation. What if they buy a house in Florida and move there, only to realize they don't enjoy it at all?

A second couple, the Riveras, say that when they retire, they want to spend six months of each year in Italy. They have vacationed in Italy every year for the past 20 years. They have rented a place in the same area every year and have gotten to know the people there.

Italy is, of course, a lot farther away than Florida, but the Riveras are much more prepared than the Duncans. They know for sure they love being in Italy. They have a much better chance of having a fulfilling retirement than the Duncans do.

It all goes back to your personal *why*. Why do you want to do that certain thing in your retirement? Why is that important to you? Before you actually go through with it, understand what it looks like. Do you really like and enjoy the area or the activity? Or is someone else influencing your decision, and it's not something you even know about or like?

Before you actually retire, become acquainted, in advance, with whatever it is you're looking at doing. Make sure the reality of it aligns with the way you envision it.

Make Absolutely Sure You're Ready to Retire Before You Resign

Sometimes people retire before they are certain that it's the right decision

for them, or the right time. In some cases, people can retire, and if they realize they shouldn't have retired, they can get rehired in the same position again. But sometimes that decision is irrevocable. If they work in a large corporation or organization, their position might be filled immediately. And in some professions, retirement is not a decision you can change your mind about.

Visualize What Your Retirement Will Be Like

Imagine how you'll be living in your retirement years. Many would-be retirees paint that picture in broad strokes. We envision the milestones that populate many retirement dreams. Somewhere along the way, though, we never took the time to fully visualize our day-in and day-out needs and how we'll spend our time and money. And that disconnect can create a schism between what we think retirement will be like and reality.

So, ask yourself, "Are my grand retirement plans enough to fill my days and my soul?" If not, you've got some thinking to do.

If you've always imagined yourself not working in retirement, remember that you'll have plenty of free time on your hands. Be sure to think about meaningful ways to spend your time. If you don't yet know exactly what you want, do a little research online or talk it out with some trusted confidants. If you need a little inspiration, these common goals can get you thinking about what you want to accomplish:

- Sending a child or grandchild to college
- Leaving a legacy
- Traveling
- Staying connected to friends
- Pursuing athletic, creative, or recreational activities
- Establishing an encore career
- Giving back
- Advancing your education
- Tending to your home and garden
- Getting in better shape/maintaining your health

The age at which you retire has a lot of implications. For example, retirement age doesn't just affect your Social Security and other government benefits, but also your ability to participate in favorite activities. So you'll want to be sure to talk to your spouse about your expectations. You may have to compromise on your lifestyle until you're both free to live the retirement you envision.

To help you both imagine a richly colored retirement, it may be beneficial to use visualization techniques to determine what you want during those halcyon days, and then break it down by thinking about realistic ways to obtain what you may need, want, or wish for. You should start thinking about your general priorities as soon as possible so you'll have a better chance at achieving them.

Consider Trade-Offs You Need to Make

Once you set specific retirement goals and begin to aim for a fulfilling future, it probably will become necessary to make some sacrifices, or trade-offs. When people have no specific goals for the future, they tend to spend money needlessly, and many times they don't even know where their money goes.

For example, if you've been spending thousands of dollars a month on a home in Costa Rica but never have time to travel there and stay in it, it might be wise to sell it and use that money to fund your retirement instead.

Think about what is necessary in your life and what isn't. For example, are you driving a car that's flashier than necessary just to make a statement? It's not that you cannot take that luxury vacation you've dreamed of or buy the lake home or pay for your grandkids' college education. We are just advising that you work with a Dream Architect to help ensure that you are measuring

your rate of success versus leaving things to chance. Remember, every financial decision you make needs to align with your ultimate goal.

Think about your current lifestyle. What are some things you could do without, or cut back on, to invest more in your future? For each item you list, estimate how much money you could save each year by getting rid of that expense or cutting back on it.

Expense You Could Reconsider	Estimated Annual Savings
_____	_____
_____	_____
_____	_____
_____	_____
_____	_____

Your Dream Architect Can Be Your Coach

Working with a professional coach, you can achieve far more than you can on your own, and faster.

Many of us have great expectations for a wonderful retirement with unprecedented freedom and the potential to achieve our aspirations. The reality is that retirement brings monumental change and adjustment. We leave our jobs, our identities change, and we lose our paychecks. Relationships change, we may move to a new community, and our daily schedules are different. No wonder our expectations sometimes collide with reality!

Retirement coaching can help ease you through the transition to create the dream you want your retirement to be. A Dream Architect can be your retirement coach.

Coaching helps you clarify your dream, make a plan, and put it into motion. It addresses both financial and non-financial aspects of retirement. And your coaching sessions are always confidential and tailored to your unique situation.

Here are some retirement topics you can explore through retirement coaching—either with us or with another coach:

- Besides finances, what will make my retirement successful?

- What is my vision for retirement?
- Where should I live? Should I sell my house? Should I move?
- What if I really like working? What are my options?
- What kind of activities am I attracted to?

Develop Good Habits

As we're writing this book, the 2016 Olympics are taking place in Rio de Janeiro. Just think of all the sacrifices Olympic athletes have to make every day. They might want to eat a few slices of pizza, but they have to follow a regimented diet to stay in optimum health. They might want to sleep in, but they have to get up early to exercise and practice their sport to stay competitive. And they might want to go to the parties their friends are going to, but then they will face the temptation to drink, eat poorly, and stay out too late, which makes it more difficult to get up early and be in top form while training the next day.

> **Your prize is the retirement you can't wait to wake up to.**

Every single day, many times a day, Olympic athletes prioritize what's important to them because they are striving for the ultimate goal of being the best in their sport and winning a medal. Once they have established that goal, it becomes much easier to say no to the daily temptations and keep their eyes on the prize. Your prize is the retirement you can't wait to wake up to.

You don't want your retirement plan to be like the typical New Year's resolution; you want it to be like training for the Olympics. With the New Year's resolution mind-set, people resolve to achieve grandiose goals for the year, but by January 5th, they've already given up. To live like an Olympian, once you set your goal, do everything you need to do every day to make it happen.

Defining your goals might require you to adjust your habits. If you've been doing something a certain way for years, you might need to do it differently once you realize what your goals are and why they are important for your future.

Although the path to a fulfilling, confident retirement is not always easy, we have created enough retirement plans to know what a lot of those habits are. We will help you adopt them so that you can accomplish your own specific retirement dreams.

When setting life goals, we must make it a habit to say no to the unnecessary extras and yes to a more fulfilling future. Until you break the chain of bad habits, you're always going to do what you've always done, and you're always going to get the same results. The definition of insanity is doing the same thing over and over, expecting different results. So stop the insanity and remember that to get different results, you have to do it differently.

Some experts in behavior change say the key to forming good habits is repetition—doing the new activity over and over again, to the point where it becomes automatic.

Christine Whelan, PhD, is a public sociologist at the University of Wisconsin–Madison and is an expert with AARP's Life Reimagined Institute who studies happiness, human ecology, and habits. She says that when you set a goal, such as "I'm going to go to the gym three times a week," it's important to identify what you *will no longer do* during that time. What *isn't* going to happen once you start going to the gym?[14] So if you decide you are going to save an additional $500 per month, you then need to decide what you will *no longer spend money on* each month.

Whelan also recommends making one change at a time instead of trying to make a lot of different changes at once, and she recommends setting specific goals instead of general goals. Automating your habits is another strategy she recommends. This could include having automatic deductions taken out of your paycheck to cover a 401(k) retirement contribution or having money deposited into your savings account. Whelan estimates that it takes 90 days to develop a habit to the point where you don't have to think about doing it. And the longer you stick with a new activity, the more likely you are to make it a habit.[15]

14. Brigid Schulte, "How to Build Good Habits—And Actually Make Them Stick," March 2, 2015, *The Washington Post* website, https://www.washingtonpost.com/news/inspired-life/wp/2015/03/02/expert-ten-super-smart-ways-to-build-good-habits-and-make-them-stick/.
15. Ibid.

Once you have determined what you want to accomplish and what it will take to get there, find an accountability partner to help you stay on track. Find someone you are comfortable talking about your personal and financial life with, and ask him or her to notice, and mention, when you are doing things that do not align with your goals. You can do the same for him or her, and you can keep one another focused on your goals.

Start your day by going through an exercise like those in the DarrenDaily daily mentoring website at http://www.darrendaily.com/ or setting up a routine like the one described in the book *The Miracle Morning* by Hal Elrod. These are just a few ways to kick-start your day with the right mind-set.

Remove Emotion from Financial Decisions

People often get emotional when events happen that are beyond their control, and they make foolish decisions that can derail their plans.

For example, when United Kingdom voters decided to leave the European Union on June 24, 2016, the vote caused ripple effects worldwide. "Brexit," an abbreviation for "British exit," prompted a selloff that *The Wall Street Journal* reported "extended steep falls...threatening to undo a rally that has lifted emerging markets since the end of January." The article also said Brexit was "raising uncertainty about global growth and pushing investors into assets they see as safe, such as the US dollar. The dollar's gains then feed back into concerns about emerging markets, making their greenback-denominated debt and the commodities they sell more expensive."[16]

But, as often happens after a market downturn, there was a rally. Five days after Brexit, *Forbes* reported that "US stocks climbed sharply for a second-straight session Wednesday, nearly erasing the two-day slide caused by the Brexit vote last week." The article reported that the Dow Jones Industrial Average rose 285 points to 17,695, and "similar rallies occurred in Asian and European stocks bouncing back from their own heavy losses."[17]

A June 29, 2016, Bloomberg article described the stock-market rally as follows: "With the S&P 500 Index posting its strongest two-day climb in four months, tension eased over the impact of the UK's exit from the European Union (EU). Fears that Britain's EU withdrawal will further stymie global growth continued to ebb, soothed by speculation policy makers will counter the effects. Energy shares capped their best two days since March as crude jumped. A Goldman Sachs Group Inc. basket of the most

16. Georgi Kantchev, "Brexit Effect Ripples Through Emerging Markets," June 27, 2016, *The Wall Street Journal* website, http://www.wsj.com/articles/brexit-effect-ripples-through-emerging-markets-1467033481.
17. Shreya Agarwal, "Brexit Boomerang: Stocks Rally Back as Fears Recede," June 29, 2016, *Forbes* website, http://www.forbes.com/sites/shreyaagarwal/2016/06/29/brexit-boomerang-stocks-rally-back-to-pre-vote-levels/#49d05fa153e8.

shorted shares in the Russell 3000 Index saw its biggest surge since 2009, while the Dow Jones Industrial Average stretched its rebound to more than 550 points since Monday's close."[18]

This is an example of a situation in which the markets went down and then bounced right back up. By taking the emotion out of a decision, you're continuing to focus on your 30-year plan, as opposed to making a decision based on something that happened in a three-day period.

Many investors got scared because of all the media reports and the uncertainty. They reacted in the short term in a way that had negative consequences for their long-term plans. When events like this happen, people get emotional instead of rational. But if you do the planning and you have a Dream Architect guiding you, you will probably react to the situation with a calmer approach. If you know your path and time frames, you will be less likely to get distracted and make an unwise decision about your finances. Having a plan helps give you clarity about the decisions you need to make.

Even the most focused, steadfast investors can lose sight of everything they've planned for when the market experiences a significant shift. Letting emotion affect your financial decisions is never a good idea. That's why we have built in some processes that can help remove emotion from the equation.

Define Your Resistance Level for Market Declines

For example, when we meet with clients, one of the key things we learn about them is their resistance level—in other words, how much of a decline in the market they can tolerate before changing their investment mix. We know the markets are going to be volatile, so in any six-month period of time, we want to know what is the amount of decrease that particular client's portfolio can sustain before she gets out of an investment. We use a program to calculate the client's tolerance, and then we design his or her portfolio to match that level.

Clients agree in advance that in any six-month period of time, they will not make any changes to their portfolio unless that particular investment reaches the level they specified.

So then, when the market takes a tumble and the client is saying she wants to get out of an investment, we remind her what we discussed a few months earlier. We'll say, "Remember? When we went through this, you said you could take a 9 percent decline, and the market is at a 7.4 percent decline. This investment could go down another couple of percentage points before you should get nervous."

18. Dani Burger and Bailey Lipschultz, "US Stocks Rally as Anxiety Diminishes Over UK Brexit Impact," June 29, 2016, Bloomberg website, http://www.bloomberg.com/news/articles/2016-06-29/u-s-index-futures-rise-with-global-stocks-on-policy-action-bets.

It's just another way we remind clients to focus on what they said was important. It helps us keep them from getting distracted by a current event, a market shift, a comment somebody makes to them, or something they read or heard.

Surround Yourself with Positive, Supportive People

As the Law of Attraction states, you will bring positive experiences into your life by focusing on positive thoughts. Your mind is extremely powerful; what you think about will actually happen. We have proven that many times in our office. I have worked with people who didn't believe that, but over time, as we've worked together to set audacious goals that have come to fruition, it has made believers out of these people. That is why we talk so much about thinking positive and surrounding yourself with positive people.

One way to stay focused is to spend time with positive people who will give you the right type of reinforcement. Avoid spending time with the people whose New Year's resolution is to work out at the gym five times a week but haven't even gone once by the time February 1 rolls around. Strengthen your personal resolve to resist the temptations. When someone encourages you to invest in a new startup that is not part of your spending plan, remind yourself, "My retirement, my future, is more important than this."

Here are some general guidelines we use a lot to remind ourselves and others of the importance of positive influences:

1. Surround yourself with positive, upbeat people—and return the favor.

2. Become more optimistic in the way you think and speak...stop the negative self-talk.

3. If you're irritated with your spouse, partner, child, or other loved one, think back to the last time you shared a laugh or special moment and how that felt.

4. Find joy in your work. Think of an aspect that is personally satisfying, and focus on that.

5. Deal with the situations you can control, and try to accept (or at least not worry about) those you can't. Be proactive when possible; this will help you deal with the situations that are out of your control.

6. Put things in perspective. Life may take you on difficult paths, so try to find the adventure in each journey.

7. Every day, write down three positive things that happened that day, as well as a reason why you think those good things happened. Be sure to express gratitude in all that you do.

8. Small, smart choices + consistency + time = radical difference.

Strive to Improve Your Future, Whatever Your Age

Age is an important factor in retirement planning. The younger you are when you begin planning for retirement, the more years you have to accumulate wealth and take advantage of compound interest. If you are only five years from retirement, you have less time to build your assets than someone just beginning a career.

But if you haven't done as much saving as you wish you had, don't worry. There are still strategies we can use to optimize your retirement. Even if you have already reached the distribution phase of retirement, there are ways to optimize your savings to help make your money last longer.

If you're 75 and you're going to live to be 90, you're still going to live to be 90 whether you do this proper planning or not. So why not make the next 15 years better, since you're going to live them anyway? If you could do anything to make improvements, wouldn't it be important to do so and make the last years of your life even better?

My mom is a great example of this. She says, "I'm seventy-seven years old, so why should I do that?" My thought is always, "Well, why *not*?!"

I tell her, "Well, you're going to be seventy-eight next year anyway, aren't you? So you might as well make it as good as you can."

It's all about having the right mind-set and realizing that you can make some improvements to your future. It's a big present to yourself. And in the unlikely event that you discover no improvements can be made after all, well, you haven't lost anything by trying. Even if you do fail somehow, we believe that one of the greatest gifts of failure is the knowledge that failure is never final—unless we choose to give up. So don't give up!

We want you to use the retirement planning process to optimize your savings and give you confidence as you enter what can be the most rewarding time of your life.

Chapter 3 Summary

Next Steps to Your Dream Retirement

Take these important steps to gain clarity about your retirement goals in our ever-changing world:

1. Set SMART goals—goals that are specific, measurable, achievable, realistic, and time-based.

2. Determine and write down the answer to this question, which is the most important question to ask yourself about retirement: "What am I retiring *from*, and what am I retiring *to*?"

3. Whether you are searching for a financial advisor for the first time or seeking a second opinion about your retirement planning, find a Dream Architect—a compassionate financial advisor who specializes

in retirement planning and cares about your dreams for the future. Make several copies of the Checklist for Interviewing Dream Architects in this chapter. Schedule appointments with several potential advisors, and complete a checklist for every advisor you interview. Then compare your results to see which one scored the highest on the list of nine ideal characteristics of a Dream Architect.

4. Write down what you want to do in retirement—your bucket list—and dream big! Close your eyes, and imagine the possibilities. Think about what you're good at, what you enjoy doing, and what you've always wanted to try. What do you need to do to feel fulfilled?

5. Do a practice run. Do a little bit of what you defined as your retirement dreams, and see if those activities are realistic and sustainable for you during your 60s and beyond.

6. Decide what trade-offs you will need to make to bring the dreams to reality. In other words, how can you prioritize what is most important and act on those that matter the most *first*? Start changing any life habits that could stand in the way of achieving your retirement dreams. Do things a new way until they become second nature to you.

7. Consider hiring a retirement coach. If you have already hired a Dream Architect, he or she will be your retirement coach.

8. Remove emotion from your financial decisions. Make decisions based on logic and your goals for the future.

9. Define your resistance level for market declines. For example, how much of a decline in the stock market—say, 10 percent--can you tolerate before you change investments?

10. Look for improvements you can make in your retirement, regardless of your age.

11. Go to our website at www.sweetfinancial.com and check out our homepage video to add some inspiration to your day.

CHAPTER 4
Distribution: When It's Time to Pay Yourself

"There's an old saying in football: 'The score at half-time is irrelevant. Give me the score at the end of the game, and then I'll tell you who won.' It's the same with retirement. It's what you keep that counts, after taxes. The retirement game is won by managing taxes in the distribution phase—the second half of the game."

—Ed Slott, CPA
Retirement Expert
and Founder of
www.irahelp.com

One of the most important and misunderstood aspects of retirement planning is *distribution*. It is critical to work with a Dream Architect who understands the distribution phase of retirement.

When people discuss retirement, it is almost always about the *accumulation* phase of retirement—saving money during your working years to live on when you retire. People rarely discuss the *distribution* phase of retirement, which is just as important—and much more complicated. That is when you begin taking money out of your retirement accounts to live on once you are no longer working. This includes all of your investments and accounts, such as bank accounts—not just retirement accounts like IRAs and 401(k) plans.

Most people who attempt distribution on their own have never done it before, so they don't even know the questions to ask or potential problems to be aware of. If you know the potential pitfalls, you can address them before they become problems.

Mistakes that are made during the distribution phase are often irreversible because by then, you do not have time to go back and earn more money. Even worse is when something is done wrong with taxes that cannot be corrected in the distribution phase. In our experience, about 90 percent of the mistakes we see clients make are in the distribution phase of retirement.

The accumulation part of the equation is pretty simple. You decide how much you're going to save each year and build a diversified portfolio, and then it's more or less on autopilot. If you have a retirement plan through work, for example, then a deduction is automatically taken out of your paycheck each month. There isn't much to do from a tax perspective in that situation. You are taxed on your wages, so there isn't much flexibility, and there aren't many decisions to be made.

For that reason, you can't really mess up the accumulation phase other than not saving money, not having properly diversified investments, or making emotion-based financial decisions. (Keep in mind that investing in different mutual funds or exchange-traded funds [ETFs] doesn't mean your portfolio is well diversified if those investments contain many of the same types of securities. There is an art and science to diversification.)

Examples of Common Distribution Mistakes

The tax implications of withdrawals from various accounts are complex and significant. That's why it is a must that you work with a Dream Architect, especially when it comes time for distribution of your money to yourself in retirement.

The way you take money out of various accounts can have significant tax implications. Two portfolios that contain the same amount of money can end up looking a lot different if one investor makes decisions that are not tax-wise.

By taking your money out in a way that can help minimize the tax burden, you can make your portfolio last longer without adding money to it. Also, assuming that your tax rates will decrease in retirement may turn out to be untrue.

Retirement professional Bob Carlson explains why the tax burden is so heavy for retirees:

> For years, Congress and the IRS quietly looked to older Americans to increase government revenues. After all, older Americans are the richest generation in history. You don't think you're rich, but Congress does. And state and local governments also are desperate for cash and have been raising taxes. Congress doesn't want to increase tax rates, so it sneaks in a bunch of what I call "stealth taxes" that mostly affect those in or near retirement age, such as higher taxes on dividends and capital gains, Medicare premium surtaxes, reductions in itemized deductions, and more.

> The bottom line is that for most retirees, taxes are one of the three largest items in their budgets. The situation is likely to get worse. Congress and state and local governments are far more likely to increase your taxes than to cut them. These days, it's rare for someone's taxes and tax rate to decline after retiring. In many cases, a person's marginal income tax rate actually increases in retirement, and retirees face some of the highest marginal tax rates in history.

> Average tax rates are likely to stay the same or increase. Here's an example. Social Security benefits used to be 100 percent tax-free. But in 1993, the law was changed. Now, if a couple's income is greater than $44,000 ($34,000 for single taxpayers), up to 85 percent of Social Security benefits are taxed. So, if you earn $1 more from your investments—or are forced to withdraw $1 more from an IRA after age 70, pushing your income above $44,000— not only is that extra dollar taxed, but 85 cents of Social Security benefits are taxed.

> What's worse, the $44,000 income level threshold is *not* tied to inflation. More people are hit with this tax each year...It's only going to get worse as the Baby Boomers surge to age 65 and beyond.[19]

19. Ibid.

To show you how certain types of distribution can affect your tax burden, here are three hypothetical examples of common distribution mistakes we see often.

The Johnsons' Distribution Results in "Negative" Taxable Income

Let's say the Johnsons have an IRA with a value of $3 million, as well as an after-tax account worth $250,000. They need $150,000 annually for retirement expenses. Let's also assume that, at this point, their sole source of income will be distributions from the two accounts mentioned. So, as people instinctively do, they want to pay as little tax as possible. Because IRA distributions are taxable, they pull the full $150,000 from their after-tax account. They accomplished their goal of minimizing their tax bill (for this year anyway), but this approach is way too short-sighted. Why?

First, after deductions and exemptions, their taxable income might possibly be "negative" for the year, meaning they could have taken some money out of their IRA and still accomplished their goal of paying minimal tax. Second, because we know most future distributions are going to be taxable, the Johnsons should have taken IRA distributions to max out the 10 or 15 percent tax bracket for the given year. Why? Because we know that in most years going forward, they will be in the 25 percent marginal tax bracket.

Capital Gains Bob Didn't Anticipate

Bob bought stock in a hypothetical XYZ Company many years ago for $10 per share. It's done very well for him and is now at $100 per share. Bob thinks XYZ stock has reached its peak, so now is the time to get rid of it. He is charitably inclined and gives about $20,000 per year to charity. It just so happens that he has $20,000 of XYZ stock, so he sells it and writes checks out to his favorite charities in the amount of $20,000.

Because of Bob's high income, he pays 27 percent on capital gains, which includes federal and state taxes. Given Bob's $18,000 gain on XYZ stock, he owes $4,860 in tax due to the XYZ sale.

It doesn't have to be this way. Had Bob known of a better way by working with a Dream Architect, he could have accomplished the same objective with no tax due by selling each year to raise the cost basis, thus avoiding tax and saving $4,680.

A Social Security Tax Liability Jill Didn't Consider

Jill's husband passed away a few years back. Now at age 68, her income has been pretty steady, so she has always known what her tax liability and her tax rate would be. But toward the end of last year, she decided to get away from the cold and travel down south. To fund this trip, she took $10,000 out of her IRA. Knowing that her federal tax bracket is 15 percent, she was comfortable paying the $1,500 in income tax. Or so she thought. She was stunned to learn that by taking this extra $10,000 out of her IRA, the amount of her Social Security subject to tax would increase by more than $8,000. That's right—instead of paying tax on an extra $10,000, she paid tax on an extra $18,000!

We Do Not Recommend Robo-Advisors for Distribution Planning

A common topic today is robo-advisors and the role they play in people's financial planning. According to Investopedia, a robo-advisor is "an online wealth-management service that provides automated, algorithm-based portfolio management advice without the use of human financial planners."

We are not against using robo-advisors during the accumulation phase of retirement if you have a pretty straightforward financial situation. But robo-advisors absolutely should not be used in the distribution phase.

They don't take into consideration all of the things you need to factor in, and they can't read your emotions.  During our face-to-face meetings with clients, we spend a lot of time reading people and their movements, their facial expressions, and how they say something— their nonverbal cues. That tells us more about what they really mean than what they're actually saying. That is a really important part of the process, especially during the distribution phase of retirement.

Sequence of Returns: The Timing of Your Investments Matters

*Sequence of return*s refers to the order in which you experience your best and worst investment years. The sequence of returns has no impact on your final portfolio value when you are saving, in the accumulation phase. But it can be critical when you start spending down your assets during retirement, in the distribution phase.

The following hypothetical example demonstrates how three different investors can make the same initial investment but end up with entirely different outcomes.[20]

Let's say three retired investors make the same initial investment of $1 million at age 40, with no additions or withdrawals. All three had an average annual return of 7 percent over a period of 25 years. One makes 7 percent every year; one makes repeating returns of 22, 15, 12, −4, and −7 percent; and the third investor makes the opposite repeating returns of −7, −4 percent, 12, 15, and 22 percent. In other words, they each experience a different sequence of returns, but all get an average annual return of 7 percent. So the varying sequence of returns doesn't matter because they all end up with the same portfolio value at age 65.

Let's repeat the process, this time starting age 65 and looking forward 25 years. But this time, we illustrate annual withdrawals of $60,000, adjusted annually for inflation, and we see that the sequence of returns matters immensely! Just how much does it matter? Well, in the hypothetical example below, Mrs. Doe has more than $1 million at age 90, while Mr. White runs out of money at age 88…even though they both had the same average annual return.

Sequence of Returns Illustration
The sequence of returns can have a critical impact on portfolio values when you are withdrawing due to the compounding effect on the annual account balances and annual withdrawals.

The following hypothetical example shows that if a person is in the accumulation phase of retirement and not taking out withdrawals yet, the sequence of returns really doesn't matter; the final value of his or her retirement account is about the same. But in the distribution phase of retirement, the sequence-of-returns risk is high. That's why proper risk management is vitally important when taking income from your portfolio.

In this example, three investors made the same initial hypothetical investment of $1 million upon retirement at age 65. All had an average annual return of 7 percent over 25 years, which followed the same sequences as during the savings phase. All made withdrawals of $60,000, adjusted annually for inflation. At age 90, all had different portfolio values due to annual withdrawals.

---

20. "Sequence of Returns: What Impact Will Market Volatility Have on My Chances of Success?" BlackRock website, https://www.blackrock.com/investing/financial-professionals/advisor-center/conversation-starters/sequence-of-returns.

As you can see in the chart on the left, all three investors end up with about the same amount of money in their accounts during the accumulation phase, even though they made different investment decisions.

As shown in the chart on the right, the sequence of returns can have a critical impact on portfolio values during distribution, when you are withdrawing money from your accounts, due to the compounding effect on the annual account balances and annual withdrawals.

*The below hypothetical charts are for illustration purposes only.

Age	Mrs. Doe		Mr. White		Mr. Rush	
66	22%	$1,220,000	-7%	$930,000	7%	$1,070,000
67	15%	$1,403,000	-4%	$892,800	7%	$1,144,900
68	12%	$1,571,360	12%	$999,936	7%	$1,225,043
69	-4%	$1,508,506	15%	$1,149,926	7%	$1,310,796
70	-7%	$1,402,910	22%	$1,402,910	7%	$1,402,552
71	22%	$1,711,550	-7%	$1,304,706	7%	$1,500,730
72	15%	$1,968,283	-4%	$1,252,518	7%	$1,605,781
73	12%	$2,204,477	12%	$1,402,820	7%	$1,718,186
74	-4%	$2,116,298	15%	$1,613,243	7%	$1,838,459
75	-7%	$1,968,157	22%	$1,968,157	7%	$1,967,151
76	22%	$2,401,152	-7%	$1,830,386	7%	$2,104,852
77	15%	$2,761,324	-4%	$1,757,171	7%	$2,252,192
78	12%	$3,092,683	12%	$1,968,031	7%	$2,409,845
79	-4%	$2,968,976	15%	$2,263,236	7%	$2,578,534
80	-7%	$2,761,148	22%	$2,761,148	7%	$2,759,032
81	22%	$3,368,600	-7%	$2,567,867	7%	$2,952,164
82	15%	$3,873,890	-4%	$2,465,153	7%	$3,158,815
83	12%	$4,338,757	12%	$2,760,971	7%	$3,379,932
84	-4%	$4,165,207	15%	$3,175,117	7%	$3,616,528
85	-7%	$3,873,642	22%	$3,873,642	7%	$3,869,684
86	22%	$4,725,843	-7%	$3,602,487	7%	$4,140,562
87	15%	$5,434,720	-4%	$3,458,388	7%	$4,430,402
88	12%	$6,086,886	12%	$3,873,394	7%	$4,740,530
89	-4%	$5,843,411	15%	$4,454,403	7%	$5,072,367
90	-7%	$5,434,372	22%	$5,434,372	7%	$5,427,433

	% Yearly Total Returns*		
Age	Mrs. Doe	Mr. White	Mr. Rush
66	22	-7	7
67	15	-4	7
68	12	12	7
69	-4	15	7
70	-7	22	7
71	22	-7	7
72	15	-4	7
73	12	12	7
74	-4	15	7
75	-7	22	7
76	22	-7	7
77	15	-4	7
78	12	12	7
79	-4	15	7
80	-7	22	7
81	22	-7	7
82	15	-4	7
83	12	12	7
84	-4	15	7
85	-7	22	7
86	22	-7	7
87	15	-4	7
88	12	12	7
89	-4	—	7
90	-7	—	7
Ending Value	$1,099,831	$0	$430,323

Three Different Return Scenarios During the Distribution Phase

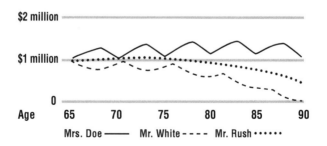

$2 million	
$1 million	
0	
Age	65 70 75 80 85 90

Mrs. Doe ——— Mr. White - - - - Mr. Rush ••••••

No One Knows How Long Retirement Will Last

A key difference between the accumulation and distribution phases of retirement is that accumulation—saving money for retirement—lasts for a finite, or known amount of time. It's your retirement date minus your current age. But the distribution phase—taking money out of your accounts to live on during retirement—could last 5 or 45 years. No one knows how long their retirement will last. So there is potentially a long period that your retirement savings need to cover.

Let's say a person spends $100,000 a year, and she lives to age 95, but she thought she might live to be 85. She spends $100,000 a year for each of the 10 years she didn't expect to live. That's $1 million more money she needs in retirement than she expected. If inflation is 2 percent per year, her portfolio grows at a rate of 5.5 percent per year, and she takes her income at the beginning of the year, she will need approximately an extra $713,000 at her 85th birthday just to meet her living needs over the next 10 years.

Retirement-planning professional Bob Carlson offers the following insight about the uncertainty of your length of retirement:

> It's critical to plan for longevity, which is a huge unknown factor for all of us. People typically retire before age 65. Though many people now say they plan to work longer, about half of people retire involuntarily and before they expected. Some people retire because of medical problems or injuries from accidents. Others lose their jobs due to corporate restructuring or a layoff and can't find suitable new jobs, so they retire.
>
> The fact is that retirement could last a long time, even if you plan to continue working, because you might not retire when you thought. Even for those who retire at age 65 or later, retirement can last a long time. People are simply living longer than they used to.
>
> According to the Society of Actuaries, a 65-year-old man has a 41 percent chance of living to age 85 and a 20 percent chance of living to age 90. A 65-year-old woman has a 53 percent chance of living to age 85 and a 32 percent chance of living to age 90. And if the man and woman are married, the chance that at least one of them will live to any given age is increased. There's a 72 percent chance that one of them will live to age 85 and a 45 percent chance that one will live to age 90. There's even an 18 percent

chance that one of them will live to age 95.[21]

Many people born in 1946 and later can expect to spend more than 30 years in retirement. Some will spend more time in retirement than they did in their careers. And there's another twist to consider: most readers are wealthier and better educated than the average person. They have access to better medical care. They're more likely to make smart lifestyle choices. They generally had careers that weren't physically demanding and were unlikely to result in injuries or disability. These factors make an above-average life expectancy more likely.

Life spans are likely to increase in coming years as science discovers new treatments and cures for medical conditions. There are many benefits to longevity and longer life spans.

But there's one giant negative: the nest egg needed to pay for all those years of retirement can be substantial. You have to save enough money and keep that nest egg growing to pay for all those years of retirement and protect your purchasing power from decades of inflation.[22]

Running out of money in retirement is one of the worst outcomes possible for a retiree. One of the best ways to help avoid this nightmare is to do a lot of retirement planning with a Dream Architect.

Make Important Social Security Decisions Before the Distribution Phase

In the accumulation phase, you don't have any Social Security income, whereas in the distribution phase, you do. So you need to make an educated decision about what the right Social Security strategy is for you and your spouse. This strategy will be different if you are divorced, widowed, or widowed and then remarried. And if you are divorced, the strategy will be different if you were married for less than 10 years than it will be if you were married for more than 10 years.

Social Security represents a large portion of most retirees' income. They're going to receive it for maybe 30-plus years. So if you use the wrong strategy

---

21. "Plan for a Long Retirement," Vanguard website, https://personal.vanguard.com/us/insights/retirement/plan-for-a-long-retirement-tool.
22. Bob Carlson, "The New Rules of Retirement," e-mail newsletter, August 23, 2016. You can read more about Bob at https://www.retirementwatch.com/about-bob-carlson/.

and don't get the amount of income you're entitled to, it could adversely affect your retirement plan.

Not knowing the Social Security limits and regulations can cost you dearly. For example, regarding Social Security's beneficiary benefits, in 2016, beneficiaries who are under full retirement age for the whole year lose $1 in benefits for every $2 earned over $15,720. That means anyone earning $47,160 ($15,720 x 3) or more each year would forfeit all benefits. In the year you reach full retirement age, a much higher earnings limit applies. You would lose $1 in benefits for every $3 earned over $41,880 in the months preceding your birthday. Once you turn 66, the earnings cap disappears, and benefits lost to the earnings cap would be restored in the form of higher monthly benefits.[23]

You Have Less Flexibility During the Distribution Phase

During the accumulation phase, you can easily change your plan. If you have less money than you anticipated, just delay retirement a few years. If you happen to accumulate a surplus, you can choose to retire early. But that is not the case during the distribution phase. If your retirement income runs out before you do, you can't go back and earn more money. The accumulation phase is more flexible because you're healthy and you're working, and it's easy to make changes. But the distribution phase is not quite as flexible, so the decisions have a longer-lasting impact.

In accumulation, there aren't really a lot of decisions to make. As you're earning your income, it is taxed. But in retirement, now you get to choose your income sources, various income sources are taxed at different rates, and they're all interrelated.

The chart on the next page shows the different sources of income taxed at various rates in 2016.

23. Mary Beth Franklin, "A Widow's Social Security Dilemma," June 9, 2016, *InvestmentNews* website, http://www.investmentnews.com/article/20160609/FREE/160609897/a-widows-social-security-dilemma.

Determining the Marginal Tax Rate for Various Types of Income in 2016

Individual Income Above…	Couple's Income Above…	Income "Type"	Ordinary Income	L/T Gains & Qual. Dividends	Wage-Earned Income	Self Employed Earned Income	Net Inv. Income	Itemized Deduction Phaseout (Pease)	Personal Expemption Phaseout (PEP)*	AMT Rate	AMT Exemption Phaseout
$0	$0	Taxable	10%	0%	7.65%	15.30%	0%	0%	0%	26%	0%
$9,275	$18,550	Taxable	15%								
$37,650	$75,300	Taxable	25%								
N/A	$118,500	Earned			7.65%/1.45%	15.3%/2.9%					
$91,150	$151,900	Taxable	28%								
$118,500	N/A	Earned			1.45%	2.90%					
$119,700	$159,000	AMTI		15%							6.5%
$186,300	$186,300	AMTI									
$190,150	$231,450	Taxable	33%								7%
$200,000	$250,000	Earned			2.35%	3.80%					
$200,000	$250,000	AGI					3.80%				
$259,400	$311,300	AGI						1%	1%	28%	
$335,300	N/A	AMTI									
$381,900	N/A	AGI							0%/1%		0%/7%
$413,350	$413,350	Taxable	35%								
N/A	$433,800	AGI						1.05%	0%/1.15%		
$415,050	$466,950	Taxable	39.6%	20%				1.2%	0%		0%
N/A	$494,900	AMTI									

Income thresholds based on estimated 2016 inflation adjustments (where applicable). Where two rates are shown, the first applies to individuals, the second to married couples.

* Phaseout per exemption

The Land of Distribution

I am in a strategic coaching class with Marty Higgins, the author of the book *DistributionLand*. Marty writes that today, people need new strategies to fend off "the beasts that lie in wait—among them taxation, inflation, the cost of medical and long-term care, and an unpredictable market."[24]

Here are some key thoughts from Marty's book:

- "Managing risk is the most important aspect of good retirement planning, not pumping up your investment return." (p. 27)

- "Nothing's going to change if you don't get started. It's critical to have your retirement plan in place. Tomorrow isn't promised, and you don't want your loved ones to pay the consequences of your procrastination." (p. 30)

- "But merely having access to information is no guarantee of knowledge or wisdom. You can read volumes about open heart surgery, but you wouldn't open your father's chest with a scalpel." (p. 68)

A Dream Architect Knows the Way Through Distribution

We opened Chapter 3 by saying that people can't give you directions to a place they've never been themselves. If someone has never retired and experienced the details of distribution—or worked with retirees who are making withdrawals from their retirement accounts—how can they advise you on how to do that in an optimal way? They can't. That's why you need a Dream Architect to help guide you through distribution. He or she has experience in this important and complex phase of retirement.

Here is a story that illustrates the value of a Dream Architect.

Henry was in his early sixties and was getting close to retirement. One day, he was walking down the street when he fell into a great big hole. The walls in the hole were really steep, so he couldn't climb out. After an hour or so, a doctor happened to walk by. Henry heard his footsteps and yelled, "Hey, you, can you help me out?" The doctor wrote Henry a prescription, threw it down the hole, and moved on.

A little while later, a priest came along, and Henry shouted, "Father, I'm down in the hole. Can you help me out?" The priest wrote out a prayer, threw it down the hole, and moved on.

And then a Dream Architect walked by. Henry shouted, "Hey, Bill, it's

---

24. Martin V. Higgins, CFP, *DistributionLand: A Retiree's Survival Manual for Transitioning to a World of New Rules & Unexpected Dangers* (Charleston, South Carolina: Advantage, 2014).

me, Henry! I've fallen into this deep hole. Can you help me out?"

The Dream Architect jumped into the hole. Henry was really surprised. He said, "What? Are you stupid? Now we're both down here."

The Dream Architect replied, "Yeah, but I've been down here before, and I know the way out."

Knowing the way through the distribution phase is a priceless skill a Dream Architect contributes to your retirement-planning process. Please don't leave this complex and critical phase of the retirement process to a novice or to chance.

Chapter 4 Summary

Next Steps to Your Dream Retirement

Take these important steps to optimize your decisions, choices, and options during the distribution phase of retirement. This is when you withdraw money from your retirement savings to live on once you've left the workforce:

1. Consult with a Dream Architect for ways to optimize your distribution options. Distribution is too complex and important a process to leave to chance, entrust to a robo-advisor, or attempt yourself. If you make mistakes in the distribution phase, you won't have time to go back and earn more money. The accumulation phase is over!

2. Ask your Dream Architect to make sure you are optimally reviewing your investments; the "sequence of returns" makes a big difference in your portfolio.

3. Because you don't know how long you'll be in retirement, plan on the conservative side. Have money available for more years than you might have originally planned for.

4. Make important Social Security decisions *before* you reach the distribution phase, when you are still accumulating wealth.

CHAPTER 5
Evaluate the Health of Your Wealth

"True wealth is all the things money
can't buy and death can't take away."

—Ron Carson
Founder and CEO, Peak Advisor Alliance

Evaluating the health of your wealth is an important part of retirement planning. This chapter contains strategies we use to evaluate, monitor, and adjust every client's retirement plan to help align with their dreams and goals.

Think of your retirement plan as a jigsaw puzzle. What is the most important piece of a puzzle? Most people might think the most important piece is a corner piece, but it's actually the cover of the box—because it serves as your guide as you put the pieces together. In terms of your retirement, the "cover of the box" is the picture you have in your mind of your ideal retirement. That picture—your vision of your future—will guide every financial decision you make.

Your most fulfilling future is not necessarily filled with things. Instead, it's filled with unique experiences and a legacy that lives long after you are gone. That is true wealth. The quote that opened this chapter is from Ron Carson, CEO and founder of an organization whose coaching program we participate in. It sums up the meaning of true wealth.

Here are 11 key strategies for ensuring optimum health of your wealth. The purpose of these "health of your wealth" strategies is to check all the details to make sure your retirement puzzle fits together correctly. You want the end result to be the picture of retirement you are envisioning.

1. Define and Follow a Disciplined and Consistent Strategy for Making Financial Moves

By yourself, or preferably with a Dream Architect, it is important to have a pre-established strategy to follow for your investment process. Once that is in place, every financial decision will become easier. It will be easier for you to decide whether you should buy something, sell something, change allocations, or adjust the percentages of your investments that go into the different asset classes. Unfortunately, most people wing it instead of having a defined process to know when to take actions like these. If you are not consistent in the way you manage your accounts, you could lose a substantial amount of money simply because of market fluctuations. This is when people often make mistakes because they make financial decisions based on emotion.

Everyone's situation is different, so we use discretion and tailor the process according to each client's personalized risk tolerance. Once it is in place, they don't even need to think about it.

You want to be *proactive* versus *reactive* because if you act after something happens, it is often too late to make corrections. We stress the importance of having a proactive mind-set and approach.

We evaluate the markets regularly and make decisions about how conservatively or aggressively to allocate clients' assets. The recommendations we make are based on the clients' risk tolerance, the number of years before they plan to retire, and other factors.

2. Diversify Your Investments

It is always wise to invest in a way that will optimize your return based on your risk tolerance, the length of time your money is invested, and other factors.

Some investments act like a shock absorber—they buffer your downside risk.

Other investments have an inverse relationship with the stock market, which we like to call "the teeter-totter effect." For example, if the stock market is going down, other investments will typically go up, and vice versa. Regarding your investment mix, would you rather have more consistency, less stress, and actually make more? Or do you want the roller-coaster ride, which is really stressful and actually doesn't make you as much? The goal is to earn more consistent returns as opposed to riding the stock-market roller coaster.

3. Focus on Your Goals, Not on Average Rates of Return (How 7 Percent Is Better than 15 Percent)

It's also important to look at *actual* rates of return on investments, not *average* rates of return. Many people don't understand that they are not always the same. People get concerned about the rate of return they get on an investment because they don't understand how math works. (Also, people often assume that just because an investment performed well in the past, it is likely to perform well again. This simply isn't true.)

Here is a hypothetical example that shows how a rate of return that appears to be favorable over another is actually less favorable. Let's say a person earned 60 percent on his investments one year, lost 40 percent the next year, and then made 25 percent the third year. This means he averaged a 15 percent rate of return for the three-year period (60 − 40 + 25 = 45/3 = 15).

Another person made 7 percent every year. Which return would you rather have—an investment that averaged 15 percent or one that averaged 7? The answer might surprise you. You'd rather have the 7 percent rate of return because it generates more money.

That might not sound right at first glance, but let's put some dollar figures with the example. If you have $100 and get a 60 percent rate of return, you will end up with $160. Then if you lose 40 percent the next year, you will end up with $96. Finally, if you make 25 percent on that $96 in the third year, you end up with $120.

In the second example, if you start out with $100 and make a 7 percent rate of return each year, you will end up with $122.50.

	Portfolio 1		Portfolio 2	
		$100.00		$100.00
Year 1	60%	$160.00	7%	$107.00
Year 2	−40%	$96.00	7%	$114.49
Year 3	25%	$120.00	7%	$122.50
Average	15%		7%	

It's a good thing the owner of portfolio 2 didn't sell it after year 1 and buy portfolio 2 in an effort to chase returns…he or she would have ended up losing money at the end of three years.

The key is to focus on your *goals* instead of spending your time and effort chasing short-term rates of return. Controlling volatility can benefit you in the long run.

4. Generate Retirement Income Without Holding Your Assets Hostage

You will need a specific amount of income per year to meet your retirement goals. We want to use the smallest pool of assets to generate that income. In other words, if we use a large portion of your assets to produce income rather than having them in growth investments, we would essentially be "holding your assets hostage" in nongrowth investments.

To illustrate this point, let's look at a hypothetical example. For the purposes of a round number, let's use a $1 million portfolio in which the investor will need $30,000/year of income starting 10 years from now. A common occurrence is for the investor to use a traditional 60 percent equity/40 percent fixed-income portfolio. This will work fine, but only 60 percent is in a growth-oriented investment. By using a specialized strategy, only $275,000 needs to be invested to generate this income, thus leaving $725,000 that the investor can invest more aggressively.

So what is the difference between having this extra $125,000 invested in stocks for 25 years at a 7 percent rate of return? Just over $634,000. A big difference!

5. Determine if Your Rate of Return Is Enough or Too Much

Just about everyone has wondered if their rate of return was enough. But too much? How could that be possible? That is not a misprint! Getting a rate of return that is too high could be a problem.

Most people think more is better, so a higher return must mean more growth in an investment, which is good. That is not necessarily true. If your rate of return is too high, it might indicate that you're taking too much risk now or have done so in the past. Maybe you don't need that much risk.

For example, let's say you typically earn a 5 percent rate of return each year on your portfolio. All of a sudden, you decide to take more risk and try to earn 15 percent in a year. Your lifestyle won't change if you maintain a conservative approach to saving and reduce your risk. But if it turns out the other way—if you take more risk and have a big loss—your lifestyle *will likely* have to change, and it could be a drastic change. You could lose some serious money, and your portfolio may not be able to provide the income you need or the lifestyle you want.

When we see that a client's investment has a high rate of return, it prompts us to look at the situation closely. Sometimes a client will take more risk

than is ideal and get away with it for a while, but at some point, it may not work anymore. If your rate of return has been really high, it is likely that your portfolio risk level is also really high. You may be taking more risk that you actually need. The thought process here is very similar to the brief illustration shown in example number 3 above.

A lot of people compare their rate of return to a benchmark, such as the S&P 500 or the Dow Jones Industrial Average (DJIA). Or they compare it against a friend or family member's. We don't recommend doing that. Instead, focus on ensuring that your investment approach aligns with your own personal goals and objectives. If you don't need to take as much risk as someone else, why would you allow more volatility in your portfolio just to say you matched someone else's rate of return?

People can get obsessive about checking the S&P 500 index or the DJIA on the nightly news or on their mobile devices. That is not a good habit to develop. Compare your rate of return against what you need to reach your own goals. A Dream Architect offers a lot of value in this regard because he or she will remind you to focus on your own dreams.

6. Do a Proactive Tax Review

In the tax seminars we conduct, we go through examples of how certain financial decisions can cost people much more than they realize. Again, it is important to work with a Dream Architect who could potentially save your time and money with just one strategy. And by combining a lot of money-saving strategies, you can achieve significant savings.

There are ways to take an extra dollar out of your IRA account and end up paying tax on more than a dollar. If you aren't aware of that possibility, it can be a big problem. This is an example of a situation in which you feel like you're getting double-taxed, and in fact you are.

One secret to building wealth without much effort is to set up a triple tax-free account. You will get a tax deduction for your contribution, the growth is tax-free, and the distributions are tax-free.

Most people are not very proactive about filing their taxes. They wait until February to have their meeting with their tax accountant and do their taxes—two months before the April 15th filing deadline. The problem with that approach is that by then, it's too late to do anything for the previous tax year.

To avoid this situation, we go through a checklist in the current year with our clients to make sure they are doing everything they can to minimize the amount of taxes they will pay the next April. We analyze their situation to see if there are some changes they should make in the current year to get more tax-efficient. You might think your accountant would do this for you, but because of the complexities accountants already deal with, many of them do not have the time or resources to do this, so it is best not to assume it will happen. Instead, work with a Dream Architect and his or her network of professionals who are proactive about optimizing your tax situation.

Here is a situation we run across periodically. It might not apply to you, but if you have elderly parents with large medical expenses, it just might apply to them. Medical expenses above 10 percent of a person's income are tax-deductible. So if your mother has taxable income of $25,000 and medical expenses of $30,000, she would be able to deduct $27,500 of the medical expense. Combined with other deductions, you can now see that she will have "negative income." This means that you could convert some of her IRA money (always taxed) to a Roth IRA (never taxed) with minimal or no tax. By doing so, you have just converted something that is always taxed to something that is never taxed. And who might be inheriting this investment that is never taxed? Probably you!

A Dream Architect can recommend which account to take money out of, and when, and he or she can advise you on managing tax brackets. We work closely with our clients' accountants to let them know what we're finding.

When we run analyses for our clients, we also help make sure they are not paying taxes on income they don't currently need and are reinvesting. This relates to Social Security. If your investment portfolio is generating taxable income that you don't need right now for living expenses, it is causing more of your Social Security income to be taxed. It is wise to evaluate whether the investment that's creating the excess income should be moved to a different investment vehicle where you can still earn a nice rate of return but is taxed much more efficiently. Or, with some investments, the tax is deferred, so less Social Security income is subject to tax.

7. Take Advantage of the "Sweet Spot"

The 11-year period between age 59.5 and age 70.5 is called the "sweet spot" in terms of retirement. After you turn 59.5, the IRS allows you to take money out of a retirement account without a 10 percent penalty. Then, when you turn 70.5, the IRS says you now have a required minimum distribution, meaning that you are required to take money out of a retirement account each year. So, during this 11-year window, the IRS allows, but doesn't require, penalty-free withdrawals from IRAs or retirement accounts.

Make sure you are taking full advantage of this opportunity. There are many unique strategies we can employ during those years that we can't use before or after that time period.

8. Use the Best Option for College Expenses

College saving accounts such as 529s are great because they encourage people to save for college expenses for themselves, their children, or their grandchildren over a long period of time. But a 529 account might not be the best option for college savings. You might be eligible for a plan that is less restrictive and has more investment options. This is worth investigating.

9. Figure Out How Changes in Social Security Will Affect You

Social Security laws changed in May 2016. Have you evaluated any impact on your overall retirement income plan because of these changes? The changes are making Social Security income less attractive for people who haven't taken Social Security yet. If you are planning to rely heavily on Social Security income during retirement, you might need to revise that strategy. These changes are significant, yet they are flying under the radar of most media outlets for some reason.

Most people are eligible for Social Security at age 62, and many people sign up as soon as they become eligible. That is the worst time to take Social Security, unless you are in poor health. You will get more income in your monthly payments if you wait.

We use software programs that run thousands of calculations to discover the best strategy for couples and individuals to maximize Social Security benefits. Right now, the government guarantees that, between ages 66 and 70, your payments will increase by 8 percent each year.

That means that if you were going to receive $1,000 a month at age 66 and you wait until age 70 to begin taking Social Security, you are guaranteed to get $1,320 a month instead of $1,000. That is an 8 percent return per year, just by waiting. Do you have any investments that are making less than 8 percent that you should use to live on instead, allowing your portfolio to grow much more quickly?

This is a strategy few people consider—they just see the ready money and decide to take it. As a result, they permanently eliminate their ability to get the higher benefit down the road. Social Security is very tricky. When our clients reach age 61.5, we call them and say, "Don't do anything with Social Security until we run an analysis for you."

10. Make the Most of Capital Gains

A capital gain, which occurs when you sell something for more than you spent to acquire it, applies to individuals as well as business owners. But because many business owners buy and sell property and goods more often, it is an area that requires attention.

The long-term capital gains rates are more favorable than the ordinary income tax rates at every income level, but for those people in the 10 percent and 15 percent ordinary income tax brackets, the long-term capital gains tax rate is zero percent! If you're proactive and are able to estimate your taxable income reasonably before the end of the year, you may have a fantastic opportunity to generate some tax-free income.

Comparison of 2016 Ordinary Income Tax Rates vs. Long-Term Capital Gains Rates

Single Filers' Taxable Income Is Between	Joint Filers' Taxable Income Is Between	Ordinary Income Tax Rate	Long-Term Capital Gains Rate
$0 – $9,275	$0 – $18,550	10.0%	0.0%
$9,276 – $37,650	$18,551 – 75,300	15.0%	0.0%
$37,651 – $91,150	$75,301 – $151,900	15.0%	15.0%
$91,151 – $190,150	$151,901 – $231,450	28.0%	15.0%
$190,151 – $413,350	$231,451 – $413,350	33.0%	15.0%
$413,351 – $415,050	$413,351 – $466,950	35.0%	15.0%
$415,051+	$466,951+	39.6%	20.0%

For example, if you're a joint filer, and you estimate that your taxable income for 2016 will be $60,000, that would put you squarely in the 15 percent ordinary income tax bracket. But you'd still have $15,300 of "free space" ($75,300 from the top of the 15 percent ordinary income tax bracket less your $60,000 taxable income) to fill up before spilling into the 25 percent bracket. That would allow you to sell investments with up to $15,300 of long-term capital gain and pay absolutely no income tax!

Like the investment and don't want to sell? Then turn around and buy it right back the very next day! You could even do it the very next minute. There's no waiting period to be concerned with. Why would you do that? So you can lock in a "free step-up in basis."

This is just one of many strategies we can advise you on to ensure that you are making the most of every dollar in your retirement portfolio.

11. Plan Your Charitable Giving Carefully

If charitable giving is important to you, it needs to be built into your retirement plan.

The way you donate to a charity can have significant tax implications. For example, sometimes people will sell an investment, so they pay taxes on the proceeds of the sale. Then they will write a check out of their bank account from the sale proceeds to the charity. But instead of selling the investment, it may make more sense for them to donate all or a portion of that investment directly to the charity. Then the charity, which is tax-exempt, can sell the investments without paying taxes on the proceeds.

In general, three entities are involved in many financial decisions: your family, the government, and the charity. You get to pick two of the three. So who would you rather have get money? Would you rather have a charity get it, or the government? That's what it boils down to. Knowing all of your options will enable you to make the best, most tax-efficient decisions.

It's very easy for us to create some strategies that will allow you to help reduce your taxes and get a potentially substantial higher net income while also making a substantial donation to the charity of your choice and giving the government less.

12. Turn $10,000 into $250,000

Here's a way you can "trick" your portfolio into thinking it is worth more than it actually is. The rule of thumb is that you can comfortably take 4 percent of your portfolio value each year in distributions. For instance, a $1 million portfolio would equal $40,000/year of income.

You could do something you love part-time and make $10,000 a year. This $10,000, using a 4 percent annual withdrawal rate, is equivalent to having another $250,000 in your portfolio. Additional benefits are that you can skip your annual withdrawal, giving your money more time to grow; you can delay Social Security and realize an increased payment later; and you can supplement Social Security if you're already receiving it, as well as your pension or annuity income.

We know some people who love to play golf. They work at their favorite golf courses a few hours a week and earn extra money being in an environment that energizes them. They love being outside when the weather is nice, and they like getting up early every morning.

───────────────

Now that you know what you want your future to look like and you have evaluated the health of your wealth, we can look at some of the steps in our Dream Architect process. We use this set of tools and resources to design a detailed retirement plan that aligns with your unique goals and financial situation.

Chapter 5 Summary

Next Steps to Your Dream Retirement

Take these important steps to evaluate the health of your wealth as you plan the retirement you can't wait to wake up to. Get your Dream Architect's help with each of these steps:

1. Define a disciplined and consistent strategy for making financial moves. Follow every aspect of it.

2. Diversify your investments. Keep in mind that investing in different mutual funds or exchange-traded funds (ETFs) doesn't mean your portfolio is well diversified if those investments contain many of the same types of securities. There is an art and science to diversification.

3. Focus on your goals, not on average rates of return.

4. Generate retirement income without holding your assets hostage. In other words, use income-producing investment vehicles to maximize your income, thus allowing you to invest more in growth-oriented investments.

5. Determine if your rate of return is enough or too much. If your rate of return is too high, it might indicate that you're taking too much risk now or have done so in the past.

6. Do a proactive tax review.

7. Take advantage of the "sweet spot." This is the 11-year window between age 59.5 and age 70.5 when the IRS allows, but doesn't require, penalty-free withdrawals from IRAs or retirement accounts.

8. Use the best option for college expenses. Investigate a college savings plan for your children or grandchildren that can be integrated with your retirement plan and still benefits you if your plans to save for college change.

9. Figure out how changes in Social Security will affect you and when is the best time for you to start collecting it.

10. If you are worried that you don't have enough money in the bank to retire, find something you love to do, that you are passionate about, and that could be a source of income in your retirement years.

CHAPTER 6
The Dream Architect:
Our Process

"If you would dream it,
begin it.
If you have an idea,
open it.
If there is longing,
acknowledge it.
If there is mission,
commit it.
If there is daring,
do it.
If there is love,
speak it.
If there is resource,
use it.
If there is abundance,
share it."

Mary Anne Radmacher
—Author, Artist, and Professional Speaker

I believe it is human nature to dream, to look into the sky and want to soar, to close your eyes and imagine the warm sands of a faraway beach between your toes, to hear the sounds of nature in an exotic jungle, to master a craft that has eluded others around us.

We all have dreams, but very few of us take the steps to turn these dreams into realities. I have discovered that the one common denominator as human beings is our desire to build a greater future than our past, to expand our horizons, and to explore the reaches of our personal unknown. It was this observation that led me to create a process called The Dream Architect™.

While the ability to dream is one of our inherent abilities, we get caught up in the day-to-day necessities of our lives and never meet our greater selves. My goal with this program is to help you look into the future and imagine a bigger, brighter, better life and then return to the present to make that vision a reality.

We want you to be the architect of your own dreams. Too often, we see people just accepting what happens to them instead of defining what they want their future to look like and then making it happen. Again, here is our definition of a dream:

> A dream is a pleasurable vision of what the future can become
> that fills you with energy, speaks to your heart, and strengthens
> your will and ability to overcome all roadblocks to achieve it.

With any major building project, architects need to find out from their clients why they want to build a particular structure. Based on that information, they will build the appropriate team for the project. These steps are important in retirement planning, too.

Assemble Your Dream Team

Earlier, we stressed how critical it is to know what your personal *why* is when you are planning your future. Why are you working so hard? Why do you want a certain amount of money available to you in retirement? If your goals are vague, you won't be as motivated to work hard, and you won't know how much money you will need in retirement. Plus, it's fun to dream! Don't deny yourself the wonderful experience of dreaming like you did when you were a child.

Once you have defined your personal *why* that defines what you're striving for, it is time to put together your Dream Team. You need support from those around you as you work to achieve those dreams. Your Dream Team can be composed of the people closest to you in your personal life, professionals such as financial advisors and tax advisors, or both. Let them know what your retirement dreams and goals are, and ask them to help you stay focused on them.

Who in your life has always motivated you to accomplish your goals? Who has encouraged you when you lost confidence in yourself? Maybe it's your mom, dad, uncle, aunt, family friend, coworker, personal friend, spouse, business partner, life coach, mentor, or financial advisor. Think of the people in your life whom you can tell your dreams for the future and be certain that they will encourage you to accomplish them. Write their names down here. This is your Dream Team:

_____   _____

_____   _____

_____   _____

My own Dream Team is composed of people close to me in my personal life and also some professional business coaches. Professional advisors and coaches can be a key source of support, especially if you do not have a strong personal support network.

The Importance of Financial Harmony in Your Relationship

Ideally, your spouse will be on your Dream Team, but that is not always the case.

Without asking your significant other these questions, see if you can answer them:

1. What is his or her biggest, most audacious goal for the future? If there were no obstacles, what would he or she love to do most in retirement?

2. How would your spouse like your support in the quest toward achieving his or her biggest dreams?

When we work with couples, we work with them as a team because we want to make sure they are on the same page in terms of making key financial decisions. But we also work with them as individuals because sometimes spouses have entirely different ideas about what the future should look like. Or they might have vastly different approaches to financial management— one spouse might be a superb planner, while the other one is not.

If your spouse or significant other does not support your efforts to plan and save for the future, it doesn't mean he or she is a bad person, but we

encourage you to stick to your plan and not let him or her hold you back. You both will lead more fulfilled lives if you're both doing the things that are most important to you. If your partner doesn't have big goals, dreams, or ambitions, we hope he or she is supportive of what *you're* trying to do. If you are communicating your *why* and living your *why* to the people around you, it is likely that they will help build you up. Plus, you will serve as a positive role model to the people around you who tend not to plan for the future.

Arguments About Money Are the Main Predictor of Divorce

According to Sonya Britt, PhD, assistant professor of family studies and human services and program director of personal financial planning at Kansas State University, "arguments about money are by far the top predictor of divorce." In 2013, she collected data from more than 4,500 couples as part of the National Survey of Families and Households. In reporting the results in an issue of *Family Relations*, Dr. Britt noted, "In the study, we controlled for income, debt, and net worth. Results revealed it didn't matter how much you made or how much you were worth. Arguments about money are the top predictor for divorce because it happens at all levels." Here are some other facts revealed in her research:

- It takes couples longer to recover from money arguments than from other types of arguments.

- Financial-based arguments are more intense than any other kind of argument and tend to last longer.

- Couples often use harsher language with each other during money arguments.

- Continued financial arguments decrease a couple's "relationship satisfaction."

- Low income combined with low relationship satisfaction leads to increased stress, which has a negative effect on children and leads to a decrease in financial planning, which could help make the situation better.[25]

Dr. Britt points to a solution: "Financial planners can help these couples reduce their stress through education." She advises new couples to seek a financial planner as part of premarital counseling, pull each other's credit reports, and talk through how to handle finances fairly for both individuals.[26]

Discuss Your Financial Future with Your Future Life Partner

We agree that this is a wise approach. If you are a young person who is thinking about getting married soon, we encourage you to sit down and have a candid discussion with your future life partner about your dreams for the future and how you will support one another in achieving them. It is a good idea to find a Dream Architect early in your marriage so that he or she can partner with both of you as you embark on your life journey together.

If you have adult children who are about to be married, encourage them to have a deep, honest discussion about finances as a couple and to seek out a Dream Architect—someone they both trust and feel comfortable sharing their dreams with. Every couple needs a Dream Architect to guide them in their decisions about insurance and investments for the long term, as their family grows and as they enter various life stages and their needs change.

We have stressed the importance of working with a Dream Architect as you plan your retirement. But if you can find a Dream Architect as you are just beginning your career, that is ideal. He or she will act in your best interest while you are in the accumulation phase—earning money and saving some for retirement. So even though you probably won't be participating in a comprehensive wealth-planning platform in the early stages of your career, a Dream Architect can get you started on the right path early in your career. He or she will advise you on contributing to employer plans such as 401(k)s and other savings options.

25. Stephanie Jacques, "Researcher Finds Correlation Between Financial Arguments, Decreased Relationship Satisfaction," July 12, 2013, press release, Kansas State University website, http://www.k-state.edu/media/newsreleases/jul13/predictingdivorce71113.html.
26. Ibid.

Define Your Dreams

Another key step in an architect's building project is to define the scope of the plan for a building—where it will be, what it will look like, how long it will take to complete, and the overall cost. As you plan your retirement, you need to follow a similar process. You need to define when you plan to retire, where you will live when you retire, what your daily life will be like in retirement, and what costs will be associated with your new lifestyle.

When was the last time you sat down and really thought about your dreams for the future? Have you ever written them down? Here are some questions to get you started.

What are your biggest dreams for the future? Be specific. _____

_____

_____

Where do you want to live when you retire? Why? _____

_____

When do you plan to retire, and how many years away is that? _____

What skills, if any, will you need to make those dreams come true? When and where will you learn these skills? _____

_____

_____

What habits will you need to develop to make it easier to achieve these dreams? _____

_____

_____

What obstacles might you face as you realize these dreams? Write down any obstacles you could potentially face, as well as specific ways to overcome them. (If you do not anticipate them and plan for them, you could encounter them over and over, and they could discourage you and derail your plans.)

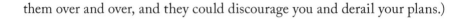

Develop the "Schematic" for Your Retirement Plan

When architects are planning projects, a next step is to draw out a schematic, or a sketch that details everything a building should accomplish. This diagram is based on what the client needs and wants—what the building will be used for, how people will move from one room to another, and what types of features will be included to optimize the building's function. They also look at feasibility of a project.

Planning for your retirement requires a similar step. We need details at this stage to gain insight into a client's plans for the future. We accomplish this by conducting interviews with our clients and asking a lot of questions. At this stage, we will review your portfolio and determine which types of investments can best match your financial objectives. For example, if you plan to retire in another country, what types of advance planning needs to be done now? And if you plan to fund all of your children's education and establish an endowment for your alma mater, how much money will that require? Is it feasible given your current and projected assets?

Although we encourage you to dream big, we also want you to keep your retirement plan manageable. For that reason, we advise narrowing your focus down to your most important dreams, and then prioritize them. Don't try to do too much. What is absolutely non-negotiable for you in your retirement?

Talk with Your Dream Architect About Specific Investments

At this stage of planning, it's a good idea to define what your investments need to be to align with your *why*, your ultimate goals. Examine everything you own and determine if you should own it or not.

When we work with clients, it is in this stage of planning that we ask them what level of market volatility they are comfortable with. As mentioned earlier, we know the markets are going to be volatile, so in any six-month period of time, we want to know what is the amount of decrease that particular client's portfolio can sustain before he or she gets out of an investment. We use a program to calculate the client's tolerance, and then we design his or her portfolio to match that level. We also determine the rate of return needed to accomplish their dreams. Why take extra risk if it's not necessary?

We ensure that a client's investment mix is tailored for his or her individual risk-tolerance level, time frame, and goals. We then present this ideal investment mix to the client using easy-to-understand color-coded graphs and charts.

The more specific you are about your goals, the easier it is to create a plan. If you identify a goal, and our calculations show that you will need $2,000 more each month in retirement to accomplish it, you might realize that it's not realistic. So you might decide on an alternative goal that requires only $750 more each month in retirement.

We like to present a lot of "what-if" scenarios to find out just how realistic and important a client's goal is. We want you to be successful in prioritizing your goals in a way that is achievable.

Create a Blueprint of Your Financial Freedom

When architects plan a building, they put a lot of vision, insight, and expertise into the project. Your financial future requires a similar approach—vision, insight, and a solid foundation of financial expertise that is all integrated to help provide clear direction for your path forward. And, like with any building project, your blueprint for financial freedom in retirement requires both short- and long-range strategies.

Architects' blueprints are detailed drawings that are precise and leave nothing to guesswork. You can see at a glance what the building will look like. As we work with clients, we use a lot of checklists, scorecards, analyses, charts, and graphs we've developed over the years to present the results of our number crunching in an easy-to-understand, highly visual manner. We make sure we are covering every possible scenario regarding your financial future and that you understand why you would make that decision. We have automated the processes we can; we enter the client's income information and financial goals, and our software helps produce a series of charts and graphs that shows how their situation will look moving forward. The interactive tools we use allow us to enter different numbers into the system to discover how an adjustment will affect a client's outcome.

Presenting this information to our clients in a visually compelling way enables them to gain clarity about where they stand now and what needs to happen to bring their plans to reality.

There are many components of our Dream Architect process, and each one is designed to enable you to discover your dreams for the future and to create and follow a long-term plan for achieving them.

Simplicity Leads to Understanding

When we present various components of a retirement plan to clients, we color-code the information so it's easy for them to understand at a glance. You have to align all that to build your dreams and execute them. People tend to become more personally engaged in the process when they're able to speak about, see, and hear the details related to their retirement They are engaging all of their senses. That's why we use a lot of visual tools, and that's why it's important to meet face-to-face.

We get much greater engagement and buy-in from clients when we show them a picture of what the outcome of a scenario will look like, as opposed to just telling them. Our summaries are rarely longer than one page. We keep it simple because if people don't understand it, they will not do it. Things can get complex, and that confuses people. If they are unclear about something, they fear making a mistake, so they do nothing. We simplify the steps we want you to take next.

We make a very visual presentation featuring red, yellow, and green. Like a traffic signal, red means we need to take some sort of action, something hasn't been done yet, or we need to adjust an aspect of the plan, such as your spending. Yellow is a caution, indicating that we might need to adjust some details if the situation continues to move forward in the direction it has been going. And green means everything looks good for this aspect of the plan, and you can move forward.

Also, if you want to see how some investments rate against other investments, that is color-coded as well.

Our system evaluates how inflation and taxes can affect the rate of return for your investments and thus your spending goals. But wait, we're not done—we then take it one step further. We know you're not going to get the average rate of return every year and that inflation is not going to be the same every year, so we run the information through 1,000 different iterations (called a "Monte Carlo simulation"). It assigns a probability that you will be able to meet all of the goals we entered into the system, given the assumptions we specified.

It's much easier to show clients where they are in good shape and where they need to take actions with these color-coded, highly visual tools than with a 50-page or 100-page financial plan that contains nothing but text. (We do use those documents for clients who want all the details.) But most clients don't want that level of detail. They want to know the time, not how the watch is made.

Plus, these tools we use are powerful because we can adjust them and get an instant look at how a specific action can affect your plan. As we're sitting with you, you might look at the numbers we're presenting and ask, "Well, what if I purchase a winter home down South? And what if I pay for my three grandkids' college education?" We can show you, right then and there, how those actions will affect your plan and your probability of success in retiring at the age you have in mind.

Below is an example of an assessment from a hypothetical client's retirement plan. You can't see the colors here, but the analyses we show our clients are color-coded. The diagram shows the probability of a client's success given a specific set of parameters we entered into the system. The red section surrounding the first circle indicates that the first scenario has a very low probability of success, so changes need to be made.

As the result of creating an optimized Social Security plan and decreasing the amount by which the income would increase each year (inflation), the resulting probability rose to 72 percent, as shown in the yellow circle.

By overhauling the client's plan, we were able to get it to a 96 percent success rate—in addition to the changes made to get it from 21 percent to 72 percent. And while an overhaul sounds major, it doesn't have to be. It could be a combination of several seemingly minor items, such as selling a retirement home at an advanced age, as opposed to passing it on to heirs.

Probability of Success of a Specific Scenario

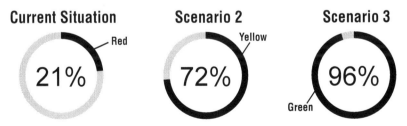

This visual is a hypothetical example for illustration purposes only and does not represent an actual client investment situation.

Our Client Review Scorecard

Our Client Review Scorecard is another visual tool that shows our clients, at a glance, how specific components of their financial plans are progressing. The scorecard shows all components of the plan on one page and is divided into four categories: Health of Your Wealth, Organization, Proactive Safeguards, and Building Your Bigger Future.

We mentioned earlier how critical it is for clients to find a Dream Architect who will work closely with other professionals as necessary to ensure that the client's entire financial house is in order. This includes tax planning, beneficiary reviews, insurance needs, and estate planning. This scorecard includes those aspects of a retirement plan and more.

To give you an idea of how this works, we've shown below just one of the four categories of the Client Review Scorecard. The checkmarks are color-coded, indicating which areas the client needs to focus on now (red), which areas we need to keep an eye on (yellow), and which components are completed and need no further review right now (green).

One Section of the Client Review Scorecard

Health of Your Wealth	
Proactive "Advance & Preserve" Investment Strategy	✓
Income Distribution Planning	✓
Women Forward Membership	✓
Risk Assessment	✓
Dream Architect Assessment	✓
Proactive Tax Review Checklist	✓
Education Planning for Families	✓
Retirement Success Analysis/Decision Center	✓
Social Security Analysis	✓
Charitable Planning Discussion	✓

Seeing your financial details presented in a visual format makes the tough decisions easier. Seeing the big picture in various formats, such as checklists, enhances your understanding, which can lead to better financial decisions.

When you and your Dream Architect have developed your plan of action using tools like these, you will find yourself moving forward with a greater level of confidence and assurance, even when there is no clear-cut correct answer to all of your questions about retirement.

A Tool to Measure Your Mind-Set About Planning for the Future

Another tool we use in the Dream Architect process is an assessment that makes it easy for people to figure out what they really want out of life. It measures eight key mind-sets that are essential to our client relationships. We have clients grade themselves on a scale of 1 to 12, with 1 being the least ideal scenario and 12 being the most ideal, to see where they fall on the spectrum in these eight areas:

1. Comfortable with Delegation

2. Relationship-Driven

3. Committed to Growth

4. Positive in Outlook

5. Legacy-Focused

6. Adept at Innovation & Comprehensive Planning

7. Process-Oriented

8. Goal-Driven: Wanting What *You* Want

Below is just one segment of the Dream Architect scorecard. It measures how likely a people are to define their personal goals based on their own views instead of relying on what other people think:

Goal-Driven: Wanting What You Want			
You are heavily influenced by others' opinions on the markets and often find yourself benchmarking against others.	Your primary financial focus is on maximizing your returns. You don't see much value in setting goals that are tied to your finances.	You believe your finances should be in line with your goals, but you may not have a clear picture of how the two can, and should, work together.	Your financial focus is driven by your personally defined "why," which is what guides you on the path to your best life.
1 2 3	4 5 6	7 8 9	10 11 12

For example, if you rated yourself as a 6 on this mind-set, meaning that you focus more on maximizing your return on investment than you do on fulfilling your personal dreams, but you want to be a 12, we will create tools to enable you to alter that specific mind-set to get you where you want to be. The people we can really help are those who want to be on the right-hand side of 10, 11, or 12. We know they will be open to discovering strategies for optimizing their opportunities.

If you would like to assess yourself on these eight mind-sets, please visit our website at sweetfinancial-1892961.hs-sites.com/dream-architect-assessment and take the online assessment.

Self-evaluations like these can guide you to discover your views and habits about saving money. Most people don't know where their beliefs lie in these areas. Knowing exactly where you stand in terms of both the mathematics and the mind-set related to your future makes it easier for you to get organized. That is the topic of the next chapter.

The Dream Architect Process in Action

To demonstrate how we can help clients focus on their retirement dreams, I will describe a hypothetical couple, Robert and Lisa. Both of them are successful business owners. They decided to sell the business and retire, and through this process, received large payout. We would walk them through our Dream Architect process and have them complete several interactive assessments. We would discuss in detail what is important to them and ask how they want their money to work for them. We would ask them to have an "over-dinner" conversation, just the two of them, to discuss what they dream about and envision for the future.

Next we create a dream collage that can help them visualize exactly what they want for the future. After we fill the board with images of the dreams and desired experiences we discussed, we ship the dream board to them. They can keep it in their bedroom, and could travel with it so they can see it all the time. As they fulfill the dreams on the board, they will check them off a list.

Robert and Lisa were already living what they thought was a fulfilling retirement, but after going through this process, they can start to realize they could be doing even more to help secure their future. Now they can live more freely knowing that through careful planning and with the help of us monitoring their personal goals, they can have more confidence about their retirement years. We will work with them to create a plan they are comfortable with and that can help provide them the life they have worked so hard to achieve.

By taking the time to get very clear on their vision for their future; having deep, honest conversations with each other; and utilizing us as their Dream

Team, Robert and Lisa can live a more enriched, fulfilling retirement. They can live out the definition of "living the life you can't wait to wake up to."

You can do the same.

This is a photo of the dream board our team at Sweet Financial Services created to remind us of the dreams we want to achieve. Every team member has added a photo or two of things they'd like to accomplish in their lifetime. Each photo shows the name of the staff member it applies to. It reminds us that we each have dreams. If we run across something that applies to one of our team member's dreams, we share it with them. Not only do we encourage our clients to dream big; we want our own team members to dream big, too. We create a dream board for each of our clients.

Chapter 6 Summary

Next Steps to Your Dream Retirement

Take these important steps, which will enable you to design your optimal retirement. These are the key components in our Dream Architect process:

1. Assemble your Dream Team—the people who will motivate you and encourage you. These can be the people closest to you in your personal life; professionals such as financial advisors and tax advisors, attorneys; or all of these. Let them know what your retirement dreams and goals are, and ask them to help you stay focused on them.

2. Discuss retirement with your spouse or significant other. If you have different approaches to financial management, try to agree on some basic parameters for saving for the future. If you cannot agree, seek out the help of a counselor or your Dream Architect.

3. Talk with your Dream Architect about specific investments that are ideal for your risk-tolerance level, time frame, and goals.

4. Make sure you understand all of the components of the retirement plan your advisor is proposing to you. Ask for simple materials presented in a visual format that is easy to understand.

5. Assess how likely you are to define your personal goals based on your own views instead of relying on what other people think. Visit our website at sweetfinancial-1892961.hs-sites.com/dream-architect-assessment and take the online assessment.

6. Create a dream board that serves as a constant reminder of your retirement dreams. On a corkboard, pin photos, brochures, and other tangible documents that show exactly what you are striving for in retirement. Place your dream board in a prominent place, and travel with it. It will inspire you and remind you that every financial decision you make should center around your retirement dreams.

CHAPTER 7
Get Organized

"In reading the lives of great men, I found that the first victory they won was over themselves. Self-discipline with all of them came first."

—Harry S. Truman
33rd US President

In addition to the financial aspects of retirement planning and the positive, proactive mind-set that's needed to bring that plan to fruition, good organization is also a key factor in successful retirement planning. This chapter offers strategies for organizing your financial information and making sure details are taken care of and communicated to the right people.

Plan Your Legacy

For many people, an important aspect of saving for retirement includes leaving a legacy. If one of your goals is to leave a legacy to your family, your alma mater, or a charity, then legacy planning goes hand-in-hand with retirement planning.

When you leave a legacy, you leave a mark and accomplish good things long after your physical presence is gone. Careful planning enables you to extend your most cherished values and causes even after you're gone. In country artist Scotty McCreery's song "The Dash," he captures the concept of a legacy in a creative and compelling way with these lyrics about the dash that appears on people's tombstones between their years of birth and death: "It ain't about the numbers chiseled in concrete; it's how they live their life in the dash between…in the dash between the first breath and the last marks all the memories of the past. That little black line defines a legacy." Our goal is to help you make the most of that "dash."

In our business, we have a saying: "Tomorrow isn't promised, and you don't want your loved ones paying for your procrastination."

Legacy planning includes a family plan that spans many generations. On one end of the spectrum, legacy planning can be as simple as deciding which kids get which items when someone dies. Unfortunately, families can come into conflict when a parent dies, especially if the details were not specified regarding how the assets were to be distributed. For that reason, we highly recommend conducting family meetings on a regular basis so that everyone knows what to expect. That way, there are no surprises, and everyone knows how assets will be divided if and when something happens to one or both parents.

Being Specific Can Make Things Easier

Too many times, people designate one person as the beneficiary in their life insurance policy, and they designate other people to receive their assets in their wills. They don't realize that beneficiary designations trump, or take precedence over, the will. That can really cause problems when someone dies, so it is important to make sure everything matches.

The more specific you can be in your will, the better. Here is a hypothetical example in which leaving half of all assets to each of two children can cause some hassles and headaches for the surviving children. Let's say a couple owns a primary residence that's worth $200,000, and they own a lake home that is also worth $200,000. One adult child lives in town near the parents, and he would really like to inherit the primary residence someday. The other adult child lives far away and enjoys visiting the lake house a few times each year; she and her husband would love to inherit the lake house. They have no interest in the primary residence.

So if the parents leave half of everything to each child, now you have two siblings owning a lake house and a primary residence together. So then they have to buy one another out of the residence they don't want. That involves getting an appraisal of both homes to determine their value. It can get a little messy. It would be easier on everyone if the family had communicated regarding who wanted which home and then specified those conditions in the will.

Communicate Your Wishes

Legacy planning is basically a plan that details how you want to have things happen when you're no longer here. Our goal is to work with clients to make sure their wishes are met in the simplest and most efficient manner possible, and with a lot of communication with everyone they want to be involved. Communication is the key. We run across situations in which parents have great plans, and they make sense, but the kids don't know about the plans until after the parents are gone. And the kids sometimes question if that really was their parents' plan. No one wants to leave a legacy that is shrouded in doubt, arguments, and legal wrangling.

Gather All Your Important Financial Information in One Place

We want to ensure that our clients' wealth is being managed as carefully as possible, by them and by us. That's why we provide our clients with their own personal websites where they can aggregate all of their financial holdings in one place and also store scanned copies of all their important documents in a secure online vault.

An At-a-Glance Checkup of All Accounts in One Place

Here's how it works. Let's say a couple has an investment account with us. They both have 401(k) accounts because they're still employed. Also, they each have some cash-value life insurance, a bank account, and a few credit cards. And they share a home mortgage.

All of these assets have values that change daily. So if a couple wants to see what their financial picture looks like in the typical situation, they would have to log in to the websites of quite a few different financial institutions. But if they are working with us, they can log in to just one financial site— their personal website on the Sweet Financial site. They can easily see all their financial values, which are automatically updated every night. Our software puts it all into a clean, easy-to-read format.

A Place to Store All Important Documents

That same software program has what we call an online "vault." It allows clients to store important documents. If they were to lose those documents, such as driver's licenses, passports, and insurance policies, it would be a real hassle. Essentially, anything that someone might keep in a safe deposit box, they would keep in their online vault.

So if we have a client who is traveling internationally and loses her passport, she can go to her phone or to an Internet kiosk at an airport, for example, and access it.

This vaulting feature makes it easy for people to remember where all of their legal documents are. We have worked with people who wanted to access an important document but couldn't remember where it was. Is it in the safe deposit box at the bank? Is it at my office at work? Is it in the file cabinet in my home office, or is it in that large pile of stuff on top of the file cabinet?

Easy Access to Documents if Someone Dies

This makes it easy for people who are living, but it is also a big benefit to the survivors when someone dies. If someone hasn't communicated with his or her children and then dies, with this feature, the children know everything is in one place—the online vault in their parents' website we created. They don't have to try to figure out which investments their parents had or the passwords.

We have seen some people go to great lengths to find documents that were scattered in many different places, or buried in boxes in a basement. Having everything in one safe location, accessible online, eliminates all those potential issues. Also, it is extremely helpful to have these important documents in a digital form if the originals are destroyed in a fire, flood, hurricane, or tornado. Replacing those documents will be much simpler if you have copies of the originals.

Make Sure Your Risk Score Matches on All Your Investments

Another element of having your financial life organized is to ensure that your risk score matches on all your investments. Ideally, you will keep all your investments with one financial advisor. But sometimes people have investments with two or more advisors. When that happens, there might not be good communication regarding the way the investments are handled.

When we manage clients' portfolios, we work with them to determine their risk tolerance, or how much market volatility they can withstand in their portfolios in a six-month period. When we know a client's risk score, we know how much market fluctuation the portfolio can withstand before we recommend making a financial move. But if a client has investments with another advisor, we don't know if those investments are being handled similarly.

By having all of your investments aggregated, or linked, we can improve the communication and the investment process to ensure that all your investments are working in concert with one another. We can make sure your risk score is taken into consideration with all of your investments.

Optimize Your 401(k) Plan

For many people, their 401(k) retirement savings plan through their employer is their biggest retirement asset. It is an extremely convenient way to save money—deductions are taken out of your paychecks, so you don't really miss the money. It's an even wiser investment if your employer matches your contribution. Unfortunately, we see a lot of people whose employers provide a matching contribution, but they do not take advantage of the match. That is a lot of potential retirement savings they're missing out on!

When you start a new job, chances are, a consultant comes to your company once a year and spends one hour giving an overview of the 401(k) plan and the various levels of investments—from conservative to aggressive. After that, people rarely visit the website to reallocate those investment choices to match their changing financial situations.

We want to make sure that your 401(k) plan at work integrates well with your other investments and that your investment mix is ideal for your situation. Because your employer's plan administrator controls your 401(k) plan, we cannot manage it like we do your other investments. But we can still consult you about it and help you optimize your 401(k) plan. We can help you make the most of what is likely a sizable asset in your overall financial plan.

One of the ways we do that is by using an evaluation process that looks at 11 different criteria for every single investment you have. Like our other color-coded worksheets, this tool indicates which of your investments are in good shape (green, like the "go" portion of a traffic light), which ones need a closer look (like the yellow, or caution light), and which ones we need to stop and reevaluate (like the red light, which tells you to stop).

We assign a color to each investment in your 401(k) plan for a certain time period, whether it's for the quarter, a year, or a three- or five-year period. This enables us to tell, at a glance, how every one of your investments is doing relative to your overall peer group. We also can assess whether the risk within your 401(k) plan is appropriate for your personal risk tolerance, the number of years before you retire, and your retirement goals.

How Your 401(k) Can Grow Exponentially

Once people see how a 401(k) plan can grow over time, they wish they had started contributing sooner, and contributing more.

Let's say you contribute $1 to your 401(k) plan. Because you get a tax deduction, it costs you only 75 cents. Now, let's say this $1 gets a 50 percent match from your employer and then grows by 10 percent that first year. Voilà! You've turned 75 cents into $1.65…that's a 120 percent rate of return!

1. Little Changes Can Make a Huge Difference Over Time

A 401(k) is typically a long-term asset, so you're going to be investing in it for 10 to 40 years. If you make a mistake and realize later that you could have gotten an extra 1 percent interest by picking different investments, it could make a difference of hundreds of thousands of dollars over the long term. Similarly, if you make a wise choice, you can grow your money over time with no effort on your part! Here is an example of how that works.

Let's say you earn 1 percent more per year than your coworker. Just how much difference will this make in the long run? Here are two hypothetical scenarios.

In Scenario 1, Sharon will work 30 more years before retiring. Her current income is $50,000, and she gets an annual raise, or increase in income, of 3 percent. She gets paid once a month, and she contributes 10 percent of her salary to her 401(k) plan. If she gets a 5 percent rate of return, Sharon's plan could be worth $495,371 by the time she retires.

In Scenario 2, the parameters are the same as in Scenario 1, but our second employee, Nick, gets a 6 percent rate of return. He could end up with a 401(k) plan worth $586,267. That's a difference of more than $90,000, just by earning 1 percent more!

2. Starting Early Is the Key

The concept of starting to invest today as opposed to tomorrow is relatively simple to grasp. But of course something that is simple is not necessarily easy, as in this case. Instant gratification often trumps long-term rewards. Let's look at a hypothetical example, which I trust you will find eye-opening.

Let's look at a 40-year period.

Pat invests $10,000 at the beginning of each of the first 10 years and invests nothing beyond this. Pat's $100,000 investment turns into $802,460 at the end of the 40-year period given a 6 percent rate of return.

Kelly, on the other hand, invests twice as much as Pat, but Kelly invests $10,000 per year for each of the final 20 years of the 40-year period. Kelly's $200,000 investment grows to $389,927 given the same 6 percent rate of return.

To summarize, Pat invested half as much as Kelly but has a balance that is twice as large. The power of starting early!

3. Your Employer's Match Is Free Money[27]

You might be shocked at how many people turn down free money from their employers by not taking advantage of the full matching capability that many companies are willing to offer. And most people have no idea what they've invested in or why. It is very common for someone to choose the same investment mix a coworker chose. They don't really understand the differences among the various investments, so they just check some boxes on the form to get it done.

Here is a hypothetical example that shows how much the employer's match can add to the value of your 401(k) plan over the long term. In the following example, both employees are taking advantage of the employer's match, but one of them contributes 1 percent more of her salary to the 401(k) plan.

In Scenario 1, our employee, Keith, will work for 30 more years before he retires, and his annual income is $50,000. He gets a 3 percent raise every year and gets paid monthly. He contributes 2 percent of his salary to his 401(k) plan and gets a 6 percent rate of return. His employer matches 100 percent of Keith's salary up to 3 percent of salary deferred. The value of Keith's 401(k) plan once he retires could be as much as $234,506.

In Scenario 2, the parameters are the same as Scenario 1, but our second employee, Alicia, contributes 3 percent of her salary to her 401(k) plan. By getting the full match (free money) from her employer, the total value of her 401(k) plan at retirement could be $351,760. She gets more than $117,000 more money than Keith, just by contributing 1 percent more of her salary! (This also includes 1 percent that Alicia deferred.)

---

27 Matching contributions from your employer may be subject to a vesting schedule. Please consult with your financial advisor for more information.

Keep Emotion Out of Your 401(k) Decisions

And, like we have mentioned with other types of investments, it's important to keep emotion out of your 401(k) account. Too many times, people hear something on the news about shaky financial markets, and they get nervous. They have no one to advise them about their 401(k) plans, so they jump out of their money market account, for example. They make absolutely the wrong decision based on an emotional and irrational response to something that happened. That's where so many mistakes happen.

You need someone to remind you, "This is part of your long-term plan. Don't react to a short-term event. There is always going to be market volatility, but are we concerned about what happens tomorrow or a month from now, or a year from now, or are we concerned about what happens in your retirement, which is 20 years from now?" This is one of the vital roles your financial advisor and/or coach plays in helping you weather the financial storms over a long period of time. You do not want to make a short-term decision on a long-term account.

It is important that your Dream Architect knows all about your 401(k) plan. He or she needs to make sure that extremely important retirement asset fits into the big picture of your overall retirement plan. Also, we encourage you to consult with an experienced professional who is knowledgeable about 401(k) plans to ensure that you're getting the most out of your plan.

Save Half of Your Pay Raises

If you were to save half of your pay raises and then spend/enjoy the other half, this can make a staggering difference in the value of your investment portfolio. Let's look at a hypothetical example of this.

Let's say Olivia does just as we advise and saves half of her annual raises. She ends up with $140,000 in savings. Tim has the same salary and gets the same raises, but instead of saving half of the raises, he continues to save a static 10 percent per year. At the end of this example, Tim has $68,000 in savings. By saving half of her raises, Olivia saves 100 percent more than Tim. And this doesn't even account for any investment growth.

| | | Olivia | | | Tim | | |
| | | Saves Half of All Salary Increases | | | Static Saving Percentage | | |
Salary	Raise	Spending Amount	Saving Amount	Saving %	Spending Amount	Saving Amount	Saving %
$100,000		$90,000	$10,000	10%	$90,000	$10,000	10%
$110,000	$10,000	$95,000	$15,000	14%	$99,000	$11,000	10%
$120,000	$10,000	$100,000	$20,000	17%	$108,000	$12,000	10%
$150,000	$30,000	$115,000	$35,000	23%	$135,000	$15,000	10%
$200,000	$50,000	$140,000	$60,000	30%	$180,000	$20,000	10%
			$140,000			$68,000	

This chart is a hypothetical example for illustration purposes only. Actual investor results will vary.

Use Your Own Account as Loan Collateral

For some people, especially high-net-worth investors, it is important to have a liquidity source without selling investments. So we allow our clients to take out loans on their accounts and use them as collateral. It can be a great way for clients to have short-term liquidity and be able to access their money without having to sell investments. Sometimes the timing isn't right to sell investments, or the tax implications might be too significant.

For example, this could work out well for home construction projects. If someone wants to construct a home, the rate has been very competitive historically. Once the home is complete, then they could put a mortgage on it. This could also work well for business owners in terms of short-term financing. If they need to invest in something, or they're waiting on some receivables, this can be a great way for a business owner to have some liquidity in the short run without having to jump through all the hoops of going to the bank.

Or if you wanted to loan your family members some money at a competitive rate, without having to sell your investments and incur a bunch of tax liability, they wouldn't have to take out a loan. You could give them a lower interest rate than they'd get at the bank. This concept is called "securities-based lending," or SBL. In essence, every investor should have a source of liquidity, and not necessarily just money in a money market account, for opportunities or emergencies that arise. Most of our clients have SBL built into their accounts so if an opportunity pops up, they can take advantage of it.

For example, if we had a client who is starting a new business and needed $100,000 from his accounts. We would send him a check. Once the real estate deal was closed, he could put the money back into his/her account. Having the extra money means he/she wouldn't lose out on the business opportunity. You want to be in control of every decision and the timing of when things happen. That way, you call all of the shots instead of being at the mercy of somebody else—or the markets.

Now that you know some specific strategies for getting your retirement house in order, let's look at some strategies for safeguarding your retirement income.

Chapter 7 Summary

Next Steps to Your Dream Retirement

Take the following steps to get organized so that your retirement-planning process is as worry-free as possible:

1. Plan your legacy. Careful planning enables you to extend your most cherished values and causes even after you're gone. Be specific about your wishes for the future, and communicate them to your loved ones and to your Dream Architect.

2. Store all of your important financial and legal documents in one place, and let your Dream Architect and loved ones know where to find them.

3. Make sure your risk score matches on all your investments. By having all of your investments aggregated, or linked, we can improve the communication and the investment process to ensure that all your investments are working in concert with one another. This is especially important if you work with more than one financial advisor.

4. Get the most out of your 401(k) plan. If you are still working, and your employer offers a matching contribution but you aren't taking advantage of it, sign up for it now! It's ideal to start saving early.

5. Consider using your own retirement account as collateral if you or someone you care about needs a loan. It can be a better option than a bank loan in many cases.

CHAPTER 8
Proactively Safeguard Your Future

"Let us not be content to wait and see what will happen, but give us the determination to make the right things happen."

—Peter Marshall
TV Show Host and Actor

We've discussed many strategies that are important in planning the retirement you can't wait to wake up to: being aware of the most common retirement mistakes, defining your personal *why*, understanding distribution of your assets once you retire, gaining clarity about your goals, evaluating the health of your wealth, and getting organized.

Now let's talk about ways you can safeguard all of your hard-earned assets and protect them from thieves, taxes, outdated paperwork, self-delusion, and other evil influences.

Follow Your Dream Architect's Recommendations

Another key to safeguarding your financial future is to consult a Dream Architect for guidance in retirement planning and then follow his or her advice. Once your advisor fully knows you and your future wishes, it will be important to stay in close contact so that he or she can advise you through major life transitions, market fluctuations, and other changes that affect your financial situation.

The people who have retirements they can't wait to wake up to are the ones who do the things we ask of them when we analyze their situations and make recommendations. They create the proper habits. When people take our advice and follow the steps we lay out for them, the outcomes can be potential phenomenal successes. But we can only do so much. Grab the reins, and help us help you. We cannot get you to your goals if you don't answer the questions we ask or implement the strategies we recommend.

Once we make a recommendation, we encourage a client to follow it, but sometimes it doesn't happen, for whatever reason. When clients are not taking our advice, we feel obligated to have the conversation with them that to get the best use of our services and the money they are paying us, we really need to understand why they are not taking our advice. If they continue to put off implementing our advice over time, it might become necessary for us to suggest that they pursue other avenues of advice.

Be Smart About When to Begin Taking Social Security

We have discussed Social Security in other chapters, but it is worth mentioning again here because optimizing your Social Security income is a vital part of safeguarding your financial future.

According to the Social Security Administration, 22 percent of married Social Security recipients and 47 percent of single recipients age 65+ depend on Social Security for 90 percent or more of their income.[28]

---

28. "Economic Security for Seniors Facts," National Council on Aging website, https://www.ncoa.org/news/resources-for-reporters/get-the-facts/economic-security-facts/.

Taking Social Security automatically at age 62 or 65 just because it's available can be one of the most disastrous decisions you'll ever make. It can cost you hundreds of thousands of dollars. This happens so often that we take our clients through an in-depth Social Security analysis. We run numerous "What if?" scenarios to discover how each client can get the maximum payment for his or her specific situation. Part of safeguarding your financial future means taking Social Security when it makes the most financial sense—not the moment it becomes an option. Have you done this analysis?

Review the Beneficiaries You've Named

Another huge factor in planning for the future involves making sure you have set up your accounts to be distributed the way you want them to be distributed when you die. There are many details that may seem insignificant now, but they can make a huge difference in the way your assets change hands once you die. You want to make sure the right people receive your hard-earned assets.

Your Beneficiary Designations Trump Your Will

The beneficiary(ies) you name on your life insurance policy and IRA accounts—any kind of documents that involve the transfer of assets—will take precedence over the people you name in your will. So it's important to review your beneficiaries periodically to make sure those designations still align with your goals.

For example, let's say a husband passes away and his finances are in order. His widowed wife didn't check the beneficiary on her own life insurance policy, and the person she had originally named as the beneficiary was not the person she wanted to receive the death benefit. This is a good example of how people can forget to do these things, but they are important, especially after a major life transition, such as the passing of a spouse or a divorce.

Do You Really Want Your Ex to Get Your Assets?

There is a legal term, "per stirpes," that is used in wills and trusts. It describes how property should be distributed when a beneficiary who has children dies before the person whose estate is being divided. If you don't designate your beneficiaries the way you want, your assets could go to someone you didn't intend. Your ex-spouse could receive your assets, even though that is not what you intended.

If you get divorced and forget to change the beneficiary of your life insurance policy to your kids or your new spouse, the benefits will go to your previous spouse, if that is who you originally designated. Similarly, if you get divorced and remarry and leave your ex-spouse on your policy as the beneficiary, and then you die, your ex-spouse—not your children or current spouse—will receive your assets. If you are like most people, you definitely don't want that to happen.

Checking the beneficiary designations is such an important step in retirement planning that we write down the date we checked them for each client. A lot of problems can occur unintentionally in this area, and when they do, there isn't much we can do reverse them.

Let's say a husband and wife have two kids, and each of their kids have two kids. So the husband and wife have four grandkids.

If the two parents and one of the kids were in a car accident, how would the assets be split? Well, the surviving child will get 50 percent. The deceased child who died with the parents has a surviving wife and two children. Does that 50 percent go to the wife? Does the 50 percent get split, 25 percent to each kid? Or does the full 100 percent go to the surviving child?

There is no universal answer to this question. Rather, it depends how you have your accounts structured. As you can see, it is crucial that you and your spouse discuss this important topic.

Beneficiary Horror Stories

It is very important that you update your beneficiary forms on IRAs and life insurance policies after life events such as a birth, death, marriage, divorce, and remarriage. Always know where a copy is for yourself, and make sure your financial advisory team has a copy on hand as well.

A recent article from *Forbes* is just another in a long line of horror stories we hear all the time. In this case, a man didn't update his beneficiary form, and more than $1 million of financial assets went to his ex-wife instead of to his current wife or three children.[29]

In another hypothetical case, an IRA owner we'll call Steve died before his required beginning date (RBD). He had named his dad as the beneficiary of his IRA. However, his dad had died 19 years earlier, and Steve never updated his IRA beneficiary form. Steve had not named a contingent beneficiary. So when Steve died, there was no named beneficiary. Therefore, the IRA custodian's default beneficiary dictated who would get his IRA (Steve's estate in this case).

Steve's will named his wife, Kim, as his personal representative and sole beneficiary of his estate assets. Kim wanted to transfer all of Steve's estate

---

29. Michael Chamberlain, "Dead Man's Outdated Beneficiary Documents Give $1 Million to Ex-Wife," February 21, 2012, *Forbes* website, http://www.forbes.com/sites/feeonlyplanner/2012/02/21/dead-mans-outdated-beneficiary-documents-gave-1-million-to-ex-wife/#5a77c7f46ab0.

assets to herself, including the IRA. She wanted to do a spousal rollover of the IRA to her own IRA, but there was a problem. Steve's estate, not Kim directly, was the IRA beneficiary. Because Steve died before his RBD, the estate would be stuck having to take IRA distributions over a period of only five years, an extremely costly result from a tax perspective.

So Kim applied to the IRS for permission to do a spousal rollover through the estate to an IRA in her own name so she wouldn't be stuck using the five-year rule and could take required distributions when she turned age 70½. The IRS allowed the spousal rollover because she was the sole beneficiary of Steve's estate, with the ability to control all of the estate assets as she pleased.

So everything turned out OK, right? Not really. She had to pay the IRS $10,000 for the "private letter ruling," or PLR, plus professional fees for a tax accountant or lawyer to draft the PLR. This was an expensive mistake that could have been avoided if Steve had simply updated his beneficiary form after his dad died—or even better, when he got married.

Also, if Steve had named a contingent beneficiary, the estate would not have been the beneficiary, and the PLR would not have been necessary. Naming a dead relative as your IRA beneficiary is a bad idea, especially if you haven't named contingent beneficiaries. Always update your IRA beneficiary form after the primary beneficiary dies, and always name a contingent beneficiary![30]

You might be surprised to learn that many people who are seemingly astute with their finances forget to check their beneficiary designations.

Analyze Your Legal Documents

Just as it's important to review the beneficiary designations on all of your relevant financial accounts, it is also wise to do a periodic review of all your legal documents.

Because tax laws, Social Security, and other important laws and regulations change, it is wise to be proactive about reviewing all of your important documents. Just make sure everything is current and accurate.

Then, once you are certain your legal documents are in order, make sure your loved ones know where to find them. If something happens to you, it will be easy for them to find the documents. The online vault we use and mentioned earlier is a good example of a place to store all of your important documents in one place.

Also, if you work with more than one financial advisor, make sure they all know if you make a change to a legal document. If your attorney makes an

30. Joe Cicchinelli, "The Deceased Don't Make Good IRA Beneficiaries," March 17, 2015. *The Slott Report,* https://www.irahelp.com/slottreport/deceased-dont-make-good-ira-beneficiaries

important change, but no one tells your accountant or financial advisor, you could have fixed one problem but created two more problems because you didn't communicate.

Optimize the Titling (Ownership) of Your Assets

Ownership, or titling, is another detail that is a critical factor in making sure your assets end up with the people you want to receive them. Whether an asset is owned individually or jointly makes a huge difference when it is time to distribute that asset after the owner's death. It impacts estate planning and estate tax considerations.

Another important detail is whether you want a "payable on death" designation on an account. Adding that designation can help surviving family members avoid probate.

Most people aren't aware that there are choices. As a result, they don't realize that choosing Option A might have disastrous consequences, whereas Option B might result in their assets being distributed exactly as they wish. It's not their fault; it's simply that no one has ever taken the time to explain the options to them.

Check the Status of Your Life Insurance Policy

When working with financial products, time can change things in a big way, and often people are not aware of what's happening. For example, if you bought a life insurance policy in the 1980s, the interest rate assumptions that were used back then were very high. They were used to project what would happen in the future. What happened is that interest rates have decreased steadily for 35 years. So the interest rate today, what insurance companies are earning, is substantially less than what was originally projected when many policies were written.

We see many life insurance policies that are about to lapse, or expire, in which case the clients would have no insurance, no cash value, even though they've been paying the premiums all these years. This comes as a very unwelcome surprise to people, especially for those who have developed medical conditions in the past 20 or 30 years that have rendered them uninsurable. If that is the case, they cannot get new life insurance policies. Or they might not be able to pay the huge premiums that are needed to keep a current policy in force. To avoid this kind of surprise, we do what we call an "insurance stress test" to verify the status of a life insurance policy and look for any potential problems. If there is a problem, we work quickly to fix it before it becomes unfixable.

Potential problems aren't always easy to detect on the annual reports people receive. All they really tell you is the current value and the amount of the premium that's due for the month. The report doesn't tell you that you could have problems eight years from now, or next week. Our analysis makes sure you are always in control of what happens with your insurance.

Another problem with old insurance policies is that some of them are based on the life expectancies that were calculated 40 or 50 years ago, when people weren't living as long as they are today.

The monthly premiums on life insurance actually cost less today than they did several decades ago. This is because, in general, people are living longer than they used to, so insurance companies don't have to charge as much. They're factoring in that you're going to pay the premiums for a longer period of time.

We can request what are called "in-force illustrations" from your life insurance company. You would need to sign a release form and a request form. Once we receive the policy, we can examine it closely for any potential problems, either current or future.

Evaluate Your Insurance Needs Periodically

Often, people buy life insurance to help meet specific needs, but years later, their needs change. This includes life insurance, long-term-care insurance, health insurance, and umbrella policies.

For example, sometimes we see policies that were purchased when a couple had some debt, and they wanted to have them in place as a safety net in case something were to happen to them. Having a life insurance policy could ensure that if they died, their debts, such as a home or business mortgage, could be paid off so that their children didn't have to pay them. But if the couple eventually pays that debt off and retire, they might not need that extra safeguard anymore.

Another situation is that people buy life insurance as income protection while they have minor children at home. They buy a life insurance policy so that if the primary income earner dies, the proceeds from the life insurance will enable the surviving spouse and children to continue living in the same house and going to the same schools. But when those children grow up and start their own families, the policy might no longer be needed.

It's important to review your life insurance regularly to make sure it still meets your needs. We can outline several options based on your goals. Here are just a few examples of things to look for:

1. Can you add additional benefits for the same cost? For example, there are some strategies for converting an old life insurance policy into an investment vehicle, such as an annuity.

2. Can you convert a life insurance policy into a policy that also has long-term-care benefits?

3. You might be able to get the same coverage for a lower cost.

4. Maybe you don't need life insurance at all.

5. Maybe life insurance isn't a top priority for you, and it makes sense to take the cash value.

It depends on what your goals are at this point and determining the best plan of action for your unique situation.

Be Honest About Your Potential Need for Long-Term-Care Insurance

We ask our clients what their plans are if an accident or illness were to make it impossible for them to work, either temporarily or permanently. The typical answer: "I don't have a plan."

With no plan in place, what happens is that people are forced to spend down their assets and then let the government provide their care once your assets are gone. Most people don't want that to happen, so it's important to plan and look at the available strategies to plan for long-term care. By planning, you will protect your assets if the unexpected happens. When an accident or illness occurs, people often need home health care or assisted living.

People don't like to discuss life insurance because they don't want to admit that they are going to die someday. And they don't like to discuss long-term care because they don't want to admit that they're going to get old and that their health could be affected. According to the American Association for Long-Term Care Insurance, the lifetime chance that someone who buys a policy at age 60 will use their policy before they die is 50 percent. So roughly half will use their policy, and half won't.[31]

It's important to have an honest conversation with yourself and your spouse regarding what you will do if one of you becomes injured or sick and can no longer work.

The truth is, life insurance and long-term-care insurance are not for you; they are for your loved ones. The insurance can help ease their financial, emotional, and other burdens if you die or become injured or sick. You might be OK with spending down your assets and getting on the government dole, but what will that be like for your spouse and children? You owe it to your loved ones to at least make an educated decision about which direction you want to go. If it turns out that you can't afford any of the options to cover those possibilities, then at least you looked at it.

Earlier, we mentioned one of the quotes from Marty Higgins's book *DistributionLand*. It applies here, too: "Tomorrow isn't promised, and you don't want your loved ones to pay the consequences of your procrastination."

Don't delude yourself into thinking you don't need something that a lot of people end up needing at some point. You can save yourself a lot of money and your loved ones a lot of stress by being practical and planning ahead.

---

31. "What Is the Probability You'll Need Long-Term Care? Is Long-Term-Care Insurance a Smart Financial Move?" American Association for Long-Term Care Insurance website, http://www.aaltci.org/long-term-care-insurance/learning-center/probability-long-term-care.php.

Minimize Your Estate Taxes

There are two categories of estate taxes—federal and state. The state taxes fall into three basic categories, depending on the state you live in:

1. The state estate tax can follow the rules of the federal government.

2. There might be no estate tax.

3. The state has its own rules governing estate taxes.

Some states collect an inheritance tax, which is different from an estate tax. Minnesota, where our business is located, has quite an onerous estate tax compared to the other 49 states. One Minnesota CPA firm calls Minnesota's estate taxes "quite burdensome." For example, in 2016, the federal estate tax exemption is $5,450,000; only estates larger than this will be subject to federal estate tax. Minnesota's 2016 estate tax exemption is a much lower $1.6 million per person. Federal law also provides for a concept called "portability," meaning a surviving spouse can use the remaining federal estate exemption of the predeceased spouse. The State of Minnesota does not allow portability. Also, while the Minnesota estate tax exemption is scheduled to be $1.8 million in 2017 and $2 million in 2018, after 2018, the state estate tax exemption is not indexed for inflation.[32]

There are, however, ways to limit the amount of Minnesota estate tax owed. For example, consider a married couple residing in Minnesota with a total estate valued at $3 million. If 100 percent of the assets are in the wife's name and she passes away and leaves all of the estate to her husband, and he passes away the next month, the total estate tax owed by the husband's estate would be $148,000 on the taxable estate of $1.4 million. However, if the couple had split their assets and each had taken advantage of his/her $1.6 million estate tax exemption in passing assets on to a trust or to children, there would be no Minnesota estate tax obligation.[33]

We need to look at the way your financial accounts are set up and determine whether you will be subject to estate taxes. If you are, there are strategies we can employ to help minimize your federal and state estate taxes.

This hypothetical example shows just how steep estate taxes can be. Let's say a couple in Minnesota has assets totaling $3.5 million, and most of them are in the husband's name. Let's say the house is in his name only because he never added his wife to the deed title when they got married. If he dies,

32. "Minnesota Estate Tax," March 30, 2016, Wilkerson Guthmann CPAs, Business Consultants, Financial Advisors website, http://www.wilkersoncpa.com/minnesota-estate-tax.html.
33. Ibid.

his widow is going to pay Minnesota (state) estate tax on $1.5 million, which will be $150,000 to $175,000. If they had simply put $1.75 million worth of assets in each of their names, they would have paid zero in state estate tax! It is a simple titling issue.

Again, you can leave your assets to two of these three entities: your family, a charity, or the government. If you don't plan, you'll end up leaving your assets to the government. And most people don't want to do that.

Build or Seek Out a Network of Professionals

Another important strategy for safeguarding your assets is to work with a network, a resource team. Your team of professionals ideally should include a Dream Architect and the entire team who works with him or her, a life insurance agent, a tax accountant, an estate planning attorney, a property and casualty agent, and any other number of resources, depending on your circumstances.

We collaborate with our clients' team of professionals so that we can look at their holistic goals and objectives, all while working together to create a simplified, coordinated solution to help meet all of their objectives.

People often work with just one professional, such as an accountant. So, their financial situation might work well from an accounting standpoint, but it might not work well from the wealth management side, or it might cause a problem on the legal side because of some estate-planning issues.

If your network team isn't working together and communicating openly, then there can be unintended consequences. Everyone who is on your resource team needs to know what your goals and objectives are, what your financial situation is, and when something changes. With the communication lines open, each professional can assess how a financial move will affect one or more aspects of your overall plan. One professional will know to ask certain questions that another professional might not think to ask.

No one advisor can be an "expert" in all areas of financial planning; that's why it's wise to choose a Dream Architect who works with an entire network of professionals. For example, at Sweet Financial Services, we have access to a lot of other professionals who are one of the top in their industries, too. So when you hire us, you are actually hiring those professionals as well, at no extra charge.

Guard Against Cyber-Threats

As today's world becomes more and more interconnected, especially via technology and the Internet, we have to be aware that cybersecurity threats are always lurking around us. With just about all of our financial information existing in online forms today, there is a growing threat that hackers can access personal data and even financial accounts.

To eliminate that threat, we, along with our broker dealer, work with third-party security auditors who continuously try to hack into our system to see where we might be vulnerable. So far, our firewalls have never been breached. We also note unusual changes in our clients' financial situations and behavior.

Here is a hypothetical example of how we watch for danger signals. A single female client who never takes much money out of her retirement accounts calls our office one day and asks us to withdraw $15,000 and send it to her. We would think this would be unusual, but we would send the money to her. Soon after, she calls our office again and asks us to send her another $15,000. At this point, we would ask her the reason for the withdrawals. Let's say the client says she met a man on a seemingly safe and well-known online dating site. She informs us that the man needed money because he was traveling abroad and something unexpected occurred during his travels, so he needed money to get home. In a situation like this, we would see a huge red flag and would not be comfortable with the withdrawal for our client. We would not send the money to her as she requested. Next, we would contact our broker dealer and the proper authorities to investigate the situation further.

It is important that you work with an advisor who takes the security of your assets very seriously.

Spend Time with Positive People

We mentioned earlier that retirement planning is part mathematics and part mind-set. Proactively safeguarding your future has to do with minding the numbers, but it's also important to pay attention to all of the qualitative aspects of your retirement. One of those is, again, to surround yourself with positive people. This is so important that it's worth mentioning again.

Identify people who have positive qualities in the areas of life you want to improve—business and financial skills, parenting skills, relationship skills, etc. Spend more time with them, and spend less time with people who do not believe in or support your dreams and goals.

Think about a person who impresses you in a certain skill. If you think Mr. and Mrs. Jones are really good parents and you want to learn more about parenting skills, you could approach them and say, "I've noticed that your kids are all well-behaved and yada, yada, yada. What is your secret? How did you get so good at it?" They'll tell you they did this or read a certain book or something else. If you can learn from somebody else's mistakes, you can make improvements on your own more quickly than relying on trial and error.

It is so exciting for us to see people visualize their dreams for the future, often for the first time. That is why we choose to be Dream Architects— because we get to be a part of something bigger than us. We get to help people live out the dreams they might not have visualized or experienced if they had not gone through this process.

Now that you are armed with a lot of practical strategies for retirement planning, it's time to go from "Now what?" to "Anything is possible!" We live in a country in which anything is possible for anyone. It doesn't matter where you start; it only matters where you choose to finish.

We wish you all the best as you turn your retirement dreams into reality and finish your working years with great confidence and joy.

We want to close with this simple poem by Mark Twain that captures the essence of dreaming big and allowing yourself to embark on your retirement journey with the sun on your face and a breeze in your sails.

Twenty years from now
You will be more disappointed
By the things you didn't do
Than by the ones you did do.
So throw off the bowlines.
Sail away from the safe harbor.
Catch the trade winds in your sails
Explore.
Dream.
Discover.

—Mark Twain

Chapter 8 Summary

Next Steps to Your Dream Retirement

Take the following steps to help safeguard the future you have worked so hard to build:

1. Follow your advisor's recommendations.

2. Be smart about when you begin taking Social Security; ask your Dream Architect for guidance.

3. Review the beneficiaries you've named; make any necessary changes.

4. Analyze your legal documents; make any necessary changes.

5. Optimize the titling (ownership) of your assets; make any necessary changes.

6. Check the status of your life insurance and other insurance policies; make any necessary changes.

7. Have your Dream Architect look at the way your financial accounts are set up and determine whether you will be subject to estate taxes. If you are, employ strategies to help minimize your federal and state estate taxes.

8. Make sure that everyone who is on your resource team (your advisor, tax accountant, tax attorney, etc.) knows what your goals and objectives are, what your financial situation is, and when something changes. At Sweet Financial Services, we would be honored to be the coordinator of your retirement plan and work with all of the other professionals on your team who will ensure that you design the retirement you can't wait to wake up to.

9. Guard against cyber-threats. Be suspicious of people who seem to be keenly interested in getting their hands on your money.

We are here to help inspire you to design the retirement you can't wait to wake up to. We want to leave you with the following encouragement—and promise—from our team at Sweet Financial Services:

Take a risk.
Don't delay.
Seize an opportunity.
Be brave.
Because this is your life.
When life gets old, play something new.
Take the time to watch something grow.
Make things simple.
Be open to change.
It's never too late to start fresh.
All your wildest dreams…They matter.
And your best life always lies ahead.
So make today ridiculously amazing.
This is your dream.
And we'll help you get there.

Sweet dreams!

Bonus Chapters in Two Areas We Specialize In:

1. *Women in Transition — the complexities women may face during life's toughest stages*

2. *Strategies for Business Owners — Optimize, Strategize, and Simplify*

BONUS CHAPTER 1:
For Women Only

"I was clueless about how to get our car serviced, use the gas grill, adjust the lawn watering equipment, and so much more. I was mad at myself for not learning how to do these things while my husband was still alive."

—Kathleen M. Rehl, PhD, CFP
Financial Planner Who Specializes in Working with Widows

Sometimes we don't realize just how much women depend on their spouses to handle the family finances and other activities. This is becoming less common today, but we need to be sensitive to the fact that many older women grew up in a much different social climate than we are familiar with today.

Sometimes when a male head of household passes away, friends and loved ones discover that the widow depended on him heavily to do things like pumping gas or balancing the checkbook. It is heartbreaking to see a widow trying to cope with the tragic, unexpected loss of her life partner while also struggling to figure out how to handle all those details her husband had taken care of for decades.

Witnessing situations like this demonstrated to me the need for a strong support system for women who are experiencing major transitions in their lives. We established our Women Forward program as a result. We have helped a lot of women navigate the overwhelming realities that go with losing a spouse and then trying to figure out how to manage the finances and plan for the future without knowing the first thing about it. We know how to help reduce both the stress and worry of the process.

If your husband passes away, we want you to spend your time with your friends and family instead of worrying about your finances. Of course it all needs to get done, but you don't have to do it by yourself. And you certainly don't need to be worrying about your finances during the grieving process.

It is important to begin the process of finding a Dream Architect now so that you and your husband can begin planning the future with a retirement professional who values your dreams and goals. Not only is it important for you to work together as a team; it is also important to begin to understand your financial situation now. This will give you confidence because if your husband passes away, your preplanned financial concerns will be taken care of. That will help allow you to focus on healing from the emotional trauma of losing your spouse without having to worry about financial details.

Women Tend to Have More Financial Struggles than Men

There are many reasons why saving for retirement is often more challenging for women than for men. Many women earn less than men, and many of them leave the workforce for years to raise children. Women also live longer than men, on average, so they need to fund more years of retirement.

According to the 2016 GoBankingRates survey mentioned earlier, women are 27 percent more likely than men to say they have no retirement savings. And two-thirds of women (63 percent) say they have no savings or less than $10,000 in retirement savings, compared with just over half (52 percent) of men. And men are twice as likely as women to have savings balances of $200,000 or more.[34]

The Financial Difficulties That Result from Becoming a Widow

In 2013, the American Council of Life Insurers funded a study for the Women's Institute for a Secure Retirement (WISER). The research team interviewed 246 women age 70 and younger who became widowed within the previous five years and had financial assets of $50,000 to $1 million. Here are some key findings that show just how much women struggle financially when their husbands die:

- 61 percent of the widows whose husbands were responsible for financial planning had difficulty filing income taxes.

- Half of the widows lost at least 50 percent of their income when their husbands died.

- 45 percent of widows with $50,000 to $99,999 in savings and investments did not have an emergency fund prior to their husband's death. Almost one-third (29 percent) of all widows surveyed lacked emergency funds.

- 37 percent had difficulty determining what they were entitled to receive from Social Security and initiating Social Security benefits after their husbands died.

- 26 percent had difficulty locating bank accounts and investments and obtaining access after their husbands died.

- And 26 percent of the widows whose husbands were responsible for financial planning had to move to less expensive housing as a result of their spouse's death.

34. Elyssa Kirkham, March 14, 2016, Money website, http://time.com/money/4258451/retirement-savings-survey/.

Special Concerns of High-Net-Worth Widows

Wealthy widows have additional burdens, such as falling prey to unscrupulous investment advisors. This is why it is important to work with a Dream Architect who is a fiduciary. As mentioned earlier, the US Department of Labor issued a new ruling in 2016 that requires anyone who provides retirement investment advice to abide by a "fiduciary" standard. In other words, they must put their clients' best interest before their own profits.

The American Institute of Certified Public Accountants (AICPA) details the dilemma that affects high-net-worth women whose husbands die: "Many wealthy widows discover that they must confront underdeveloped financial plans that leave them feeling unsure and insecure. Widowhood also requires a different approach to navigate a path to financial stability that will support emotional recovery. The lack of advanced planning by high-net-worth couples contributes to this tumultuous state in which widows find themselves."[35]

AICPA also notes that widows "exhibit the range of dysfunction from super hoarder to super frugal, independent of the actual assets at their disposal. For some, even having a $10 million or $15 million net worth doesn't get them beyond the fear that they might end up homeless living on the street. They're also scared someone will take advantage of them and walk off with their money."[36]

The association also reports, "Especially with widows who are older and coming from a marriage with many assets, advisors have noted how many weren't involved with financial management to any degree." Also, some widows have "blown through $2 million in two years." And many widows are in "an emotional state of paralysis where they're unable to focus on the decisions facing them."[37]

Why Many Women Avoid Getting Involved in Finances

In our experience, most women who avoid getting involved in the finances steer clear from the process for a handful of reasons. Here they are.

1. **They don't understand finances**—Or they don't want to. It's too overwhelming. It's just too much to try to start learning at this stage of life. We make the process simple. The tools we've developed over the years help make it easy to see and understand exactly what you

35. Lewis Schiff, "The Vulnerability of High-Net-Worth Widows," September 18, 2008, AICPA website, https://www.aicpastore.com/Content/media/PRODUCER_CONTENT/Newsletters/Articles_2008/Wealth/Vulnerability.jsp.
36. Ibid.
37. Ibid.

need to do next and what your retirement will look like. It doesn't have to be complicated. During life's most stressful transitions, things can seem fuzzy and foggy. You might feel like you're in a daze or moving in slow motion. We will focus on only one or two decisions at a time so you don't feel overwhelmed.

2. **They figure their husband has it covered**—We hear this a lot: "My husband is the one who takes care of the finances, so I don't need to worry about it. He has it all under control." That may be true, but statistics show that women outlive men, so there's a chance that a woman is going to have to deal with it at some point in her life.

   A 2014 report from the Centers for Disease Control and Prevention found that life expectancy in the United States is at an all-time high. The report revealed that in 2012, the life expectancy for females was 81.2 years, while the life expectancy for men was 76.4 years.[38]

   Our goal is to make sure that we can get women at least engaged with the planning process. They don't have to understand the fine details, but it is important for them to participate.

3. **They say their kids are taking care of things**—We hear this a lot when we work with widowed clients or older clients who are divorced and have children. They will say things like, "My son Billy is real sharp with this, and he thinks I should do this type of an investment." But then we find out that Billy has no training or expertise in investments or retirement planning. Of course people give their children's opinions a lot of merit, but retirement planning is something you can't do over, so it's critical to work with a trained, licensed professional—a Dream Architect.

4. **They are afraid**—We work with a lot of women who don't want to learn about their finances because they're afraid of what they might find out. They don't know what the future holds. Ignorance is bliss, so if they don't have enough money for the future, they'll just brush it under the rug and ignore it. They just can't deal with it.

   We believe education and knowledge can take the teeth out of fear. So we will educate you, patiently and in a compassionate manner. We want to help you overcome your fears. So let's not sweep things under the rug. Let's talk about them, and let's find out what's driving that fear. Is it a fear of running out of money? We can formulate a

---

38. Honor Whiteman, "CDC: Life Expectancy in the US Reaches Record High," October 8, 2014, Centers for Disease Control website, http://www.medicalnewstoday.com/articles/283625.php.

plan that will allow you to be OK if you follow it.

5. **They don't know where to start**—Again, no one teaches us about finances in high school or college, so if our parents don't teach us, where will we learn? Most people don't learn—especially women. Then, when a woman becomes divorced or widowed, she has no idea where to begin.

It is a deeply moving experience for us to help people who are experiencing such incredible stress, frustration, and uncertainty and don't know what to do next, so they don't do anything. They are frozen. We create ways to help them move forward. Please know that there are people who are educated, trained, and qualified to help you with this type of situation. You do not have to go through it alone. We specialize in educating women about their finances and their options.

Couples: Try to Understand Each Other's Goals

As we mentioned earlier, it is really important for couples to discuss their views about finances and their goals for the future before getting married. A husband and wife certainly don't have to have the same exact dreams, goals, or vision for the future. But they do need to communicate about those dreams and share some similar philosophies. If they are not on the same page at all, it can be a recipe for disaster.

Think about a couple who is looking to work on their relationship, so they decide to go to counseling. How effective would that counseling be if only one spouse participated? One person is working to make the relationship better, but the other is potentially on a completely different page. This is similar to being involved with financial planning. If only one person is present to voice his or her hopes and dreams for their future, how can that be productive for the couple? Spouses often have different dreams and visions for their future, so it's important that both communicate and plan together to design the life they can't wait to wake up to. A good resource that can help you really go deep into this process is mylifebook.com, which is a complete life-development system for creating your very best life.

In a lot of cases, couples have

vastly different styles of managing money. For example, one spouse is a saver, and the other is a spender. As you can imagine, this can create a lot of friction in a marriage, and it often leads to divorce. It doesn't have to, though. We can help a couple who really wants to meet in the middle.

If we know what the spender wants to spend on, and we know what the saver wants to save for, we can develop a plan that allows both spouses to do some of what they like, and they can still reach their ultimate financial goals. But if they don't have a plan or a willingness to compromise, it's definitely going to be a problem because they are not working together.

Each spouse needs to know what they need to sacrifice so they can stay married and live happily ever after. It really can be that easy with some planning. But if you never sit down to look at the numbers and plan together, the rough times will most likely continue.

Helping Women Move Forward During Life Transitions

Kathleen Rehl, PhD, is an advocate for widows, and she conducted a seminar for us recently. She is a widow herself, and actually, the loss of her husband is what brought her into the business. She has written books on widowhood, and she supports other women. She is the author of *Moving Forward on Your Own: A Financial Guidebook for Widow*. You can download a chapter from that book, "Financial Steps for Recent Widows," from her website. It contains an extremely helpful checklist of tasks a woman needs to take care of if her husband dies.

On her website at www.kathleenrehl.com, Kathleen says that more than 1 million women are widowed every year in our country and that this number will soon total 13 million. "No woman wants to join this club, which is a heart-breaking event," she writes. "But 70 percent of all married women will experience widowhood, and 80 percent of women will die single. Yet 80 percent of all men die married!"

We believe that women tend to feel or react more to major life transitions than men do. In our extensive work with women, we have learned a thing or two about working with women as they are going through major life transitions. There are many ways we can help women through those changes in their lives, such as divorce, becoming a widow, getting remarried, and becoming an empty-nester once the last child goes to college.

Understanding Social Security Will Help You Maximize Your Benefit

The laws governing Social Security are complex even for an individual. They become even more difficult to understand when they apply to surviving spouses.

Social Security expert Larry Kotlikoff, a Boston University economist, writes a column for PBS in which he reports on how to optimize Social Security benefits. In one column, he gave an "extreme" example of a hypothetical 62-year-old widow he called Sarah. Here is his description of this scenario:[39]

> Sarah contacts Social Security to file for a survivor benefit on her deceased husband's or ex-husband's work record. (In the case of a deceased ex, she had to be married to him for a decade or more). Let's assume that Sarah's widow benefit is $2,001 per month and that her own age-62 early retirement benefit is $2,000 per month.
>
> Sarah is under no requirement to file for her retirement benefit at age 62. Indeed, she can wait until age 70 to file for it. At 70, it will start at a 76 percent higher level.
>
> But the Social Security staffer files Sarah for both benefits. In doing so, he leaves Sarah with just her $2,001 widow's benefit, because you can only collect the larger of the two benefits if you have filed (or been filed) for both.
>
> In filing for her retirement benefit, the Social Security staffer produces not a single penny more in benefits for Sarah. But by doing so, he prevents Sarah from filing for her own retirement benefit when she reaches age 70. As a result, that prevents her from collecting $3,520 per month in retirement benefits instead of the $2,001 per month in widow's benefits. (Her own full retirement benefit, if it were allowed to grow until age 70, would be 1.76 times the $2,000: $3,520 a month and $42,240 a year).
>
> So the staffer would have deprived Sarah of the ability to collect $18,240 more per year from age 70 through 100, should she live that long.

39. Laurence Kotlikoff, "Column: Widows Lose Thousands in Social Security Benefits Due to Misinformation," November 24, 2015, PBS website, http://www.pbs.org/newshour/making-sense/column-widows-lose-thousands-in-social-security-benefits-due-to-misinformation/.

As you can see, knowledge is power! The more you know about Social Security, the more you can be confident that you are getting the maximum amount possible.

What We Can Learn About Transformation from the Butterfly

Change is inevitable, and sometimes it is difficult to accept change and learn how to adapt to our new circumstances. We can learn a lot from the butterfly about reinventing ourselves in the face of change.

Native Americans consider the butterfly to be a symbol of change, joy, transformation, and resurrection. In fact, butterflies survive because of six primary qualities:

- Their ability to fly enables them to populate large geographic areas.

- They are extremely adaptable to their environment and climate.

- Their external skeleton provides a kind of self-protective armor.

- Because of their small size, their dietary needs are meager and accessible.

- They can delay fertilization until conditions are beneficial, which enhances their ability to survive as a species.

- They undergo multiple changes through metamorphosis (egg, larva, pupa, and adult) to thrive and emerge more beautiful than ever.

Butterflies appear to dance as they flutter among the flowers. They remind us not to take things so seriously in our lives. They awaken a sense of lightness and joy in us. They remind us to get up and move, for if you do not move, you cannot dance.

The lesson we can take from the butterfly is to let go of old behaviors and move gracefully into the next phase of existence. We all transform through multiple stages of life.

Women Forward: Helping You Create the Best Life Possible

We all face transitions at some point in our lives. We are here to help build up your confidence in your abilities to do the things you never learned to do or fear doing. We want to empower you to say, "I can do this. This isn't as scary as what I thought it would be." We want you to know that we are here to help you through any situation you face. We also realize that sometimes you might just want to hear a friendly voice on the other end of the phone, a reassuring word. Feel free to call us any time. Our entire team is great at listening.

Through our Women Forward program, we focus on not just your finances, but also on your personal development. Our goal is to help you navigate the path to your best life. We want to help provide you with the guidance, tools, and support you need to create and live your best life possible.

We listen to hear, not to respond. We want to hear what your concerns, needs, and fears are. We have your best interest at heart, and we want to help you navigate the bumpy terrain of financial details.

And there's more to it than just getting your financial house in order for the future. We want you to dream again! Maybe it has been a long time since you focused on your own dreams for the future. We work with many women who have never sat down and asked themselves, "What do I want? What makes me happy?" They have taken care of their husbands and families for so long that they have grown accustomed to being last in line. We want to move you to the head of the line!

Whatever type of life transition you are facing, you *can* dream again. Even if you are going through a painful time right now, please know that at some point, the clouds are going to part, and you can have a life you're excited to live again. If you're not happy with the way things are today, we can help you make things better. We want to work with you to design the retirement you can't wait to wake up to!

Bonus Chapter 1 Summary

Next Steps to Your Dream Retirement

Take these important steps to prepare for the future:

1. Acknowledge that women typically face more challenges than men when it comes to planning for the future. Find a Dream Architect now, and begin to understand your financial situation. That way, you will feel more confident about your future because you will know where you stand financially. And if your husband dies before you do, your preplanned financial concerns will be taken care of, and you can focus on healing from the emotional trauma of losing your spouse.

2. If you haven't discussed the future with your husband (recently or ever), have an "over-dinner" conversation with him to discuss what the future should look like. Try to find some common ground, but don't compromise away your most cherished dreams.

3. Decide what *you* want for the future. If you have always put your spouse and family first and put your own dreams on hold, start daydreaming about the retirement you can't wait to wake up to. Dare to dream!

4. Visit http://www.sweetfinancial.com/women-forward/ for resources and guidance on how to take control of your finances and build the *life* you can't wait to wake up to.

BONUS CHAPTER 2:
Business Owners, Stop Here!

"Far and away the best prize that life offers is the chance to work hard at work worth doing."

—Theodore Roosevelt
26th President of the United States

Owning a business can be one of the most rewarding things you'll ever do. It is even more fulfilling, rewarding, and enjoyable when you know how to shift your focus from managing a business to reaching your goals. Business owners face different financial complexities than individual investors. It is another piece of the investment puzzle, and we can help you make the most of your hard work, time, and effort. We specialize in designing customized retirement plans for business owners.

For example, if you're a business owner, your tax situation can vary greatly from one year to the next. Some of the tax burden is controllable in terms of capital expenditures or the timing of capital deployment. Taxes can actually be more flexible for business owners than individuals, and we can show you some strategies to help minimize taxes.

Cash optimization is a key area of concern to business owners, too. We can advise you on decisions related to borrowing money, paying off debts, and making loans to others.

Learn from Our Mistakes

We opened Chapter 3 by saying, "People can't give you directions to a place they've never been themselves." As someone who has owned a business for nearly four decades, I have many of the same challenges you do in running a business. If we can help eliminate or minimize some of the bumps and bruises along the way, that is what we're passionate about, and that is why we are in business.

Through the years at Sweet Financial Services, we have encountered just about every type of financial situation a business owner can experience, and we have designed customized retirement solutions that align with our clients' goals and dreams. If you are a business owner who is encountering financial situations you're not sure how to solve, we can help you. Because this is an area we specialize in, we can transform what might seem like an intimidating and difficult situation into a manageable process with a positive outcome.

The following are some actions you will need to take as you look toward retirement and what will happen to your business once you retire.

Decide on Your Exit Strategy

Your business is probably your largest investment or asset. So in addition to focusing on your day-to-day operations, you also need an exit strategy. How will you turn your largest investment into a retirement income stream, if that is your ultimate goal? There are many options. Are any of your family members in the business? Do non-family members own a large portion of the business? How will you sell off your portion, and to whom? Will you still be the majority owner? Will you ever get to the point where you're a minority owner?

If you do not plan to have your business generate a revenue stream during your retirement, what do you plan to do with the business? Sell it? Give it to family members? If so, when?

There are tax and other implications of any route you plan to go, so be sure to consult a Dream Architect before you put your plan in motion. And it's wise to do so as far in advance as possible. If you decide to retire in two months, it will be hard to create an optimum exit strategy in that amount of time. To get the most out of your lifetime of effort requires advanced planning.

Optimize All of Your Processes

Whether you plan to keep your business as a revenue stream or sell it once you retire, it is important to do everything you can to maximize its value.

A business can be anything from a farm to a law office to a car dealership to a manufacturing firm. What we've discovered over the years, though, is that regardless of how different businesses are in their structure and function, most business owners have the exact same frustrations and concerns. They experience many of the same roadblocks and challenges, regardless of how big or small their businesses are. Here are some examples of those common frustrations:

1. **Hiring good employees**—Especially in smaller communities, we often hear business owners ask, "How can I find good candidates in this area" And how can I interview them properly to find out if they have the skills I'm looking for—or if they're just bluffing me?"

   It is important to find people who fit in with your culture and share your values. You can teach them any kind of skill, but if they don't share your values, it's not going to work out. I think that, unfortunately, most business owners don't look at the right factors when they hire people, so they hire and then let go of a lot of people. If they would look for the most important criteria up front, it would make the process a lot less stressful and a lot less time-consuming and costly.

2. **Keeping employees engaged**—Business owners often ask, "How do I get my team engaged? How do I get them to act as owners and get on board to support what we're trying to do?"

3. **Retaining employees**—Once you get good people on board, how do you keep them? This is another concern that business owners share. They want to know how to inspire their employees and keep them happy.

   One of our business-owner clients who is very successful had been giving his employees a trip each year, or a generous Christmas bonus. He finally realized that nobody really appreciated those monetary gifts. They did not give people a morale boost. He was frustrated that he had shelled out so much money for gifts no one even cared about.

   We would suggest that, instead, he might want to understand what's really important to each individual. For example, a lot of people appreciate the gift of time. So maybe a few days off to spend with family would hold a lot of value. Or maybe some people would like to have a bigger say in the company's future direction.

4. **Being an effective leader**—Many business owners want to know how to stop spending so much time *in* their businesses, and instead work *on* their businesses. They want to know how to take a step back from the daily operations while still ensuring that the business is operating at the same level of efficiency, or even a higher level, than what their expectations are.

   In our assessments, we call this a "self-managing company." It's a term we have borrowed from Dan Sullivan of The Strategic Coach. Here is how Dan defines a self-managing company:

   > The Self-Managing Company is a company that manages itself to growth. In a Self-Managing Company, not only does the company grow when the entrepreneur is not there, it actually grows more as the entrepreneur becomes more freed up. This kind of entrepreneurial freedom, where your business becomes the vehicle for the achievement of all your life's goals, is what we're focused on.
   > It's freedom of time, money, relationship, and purpose: having the freedom to work only when you want, make as much money as you want, work with whomever you want, and create the kind of world you want.

   Who wouldn't want that type of self-managing and multiplying business?

5. **Creating a better client experience**—You can walk into any type of business and tell immediately whether or not the owner and managers are running a client-focused company. What are you doing to create a "wow" experience for your clients?

Dan Sullivan coaches business owners to follow the Referability Habits. There are only four, and they are incredibly simple. Yet you'd so surprised at how many business owners don't do these very simple things:

1. Show up on time.

2. Do what you say.

3. Finish what you start.

4. Say please and thank you.

In my opinion, business owners who make these simple but profound actions the core of their businesses will see spectacular improvements in their results. When you walk into a business, you can see immediately whether or not the business owner is following these guidelines.

6. **Increasing profitability**—All business owners are looking to do this in an efficient and effective way. This is one of our challenges as well. How can we attract new business without having to send a bunch of people out knocking on doors? There are effective strategies for increasing profitability in a more systematic, efficient way.

If any of these business concerns sound familiar to you, we can help you solve them. Go to http://www.sweetfinancial.com/smarter-business/ and take our Smarter Business Coaching Assessment to see what your next step is.

Bonus Chapter 2 Summary

Next Steps to Your Dream Retirement

Take these important steps that will enable you to get the most out of your business, now and as you transition into retirement:

1. Instead of learning from your own mistakes, learn from the mistakes we've made during almost four decades in business—and from the mistakes we've seen other people make.

2. Decide on your exit strategy. Will you sell your business or turn it over to family members, for example?

3. Streamline all of your business processes to ensure optimum outcomes. Make any changes needed to improve your processes for hiring good employees, keeping employees engaged, retaining employees, being an effective manager, and creating a better client experience.

4. Visit our website at http://www.sweetfinancial.com/smarter-business/ and take the Smarter Business Coaching assessment to see what your next step is.

Sweet Financial
services

Located at 1300 S. Prairie Ave., Fairmont, Minnesota 56031
(507) 235-5587

Securities offered through Raymond James Financial Services Inc., Member
FINRA/SIPC

At Sweet Financial Services, our team is committed to designing customized retirement plans for people so that retirement is the best time of their lives. We do things differently. We focus on helping to guide our clients to live their dreams, achieve ambitious goals, and think bigger. We don't want you to chase returns in the stock market; we want you to make sure that what you're doing in the next phase of your life is in line with your personal *why* and with your personal goals.

Sweet Financial Services has been in business since December 1979. We have designed retirement plans for hundreds of people, so we have seen just about every situation there is. Planning for retirement can be intimidating and confusing because you've never done it before. So it's natural to have questions and concerns and to be apprehensive. Let us worry about the potential roadblocks you might not see because we specialize in retirement planning. Don't think you have to do this on your own.

And remember, there is a huge difference between the accumulation of assets and the distribution of them.

How Coaching Strengthens Our Team

At Sweet Financial Services, it is important for us to invest in the education of our team so that we can serve our clients optimally.

We have found it valuable to engage in personal coaching from some phenomenal organizations led by big thinkers. When we get exposed to these people and their ideas and share those ideas with our clients, we realize that most people just don't know this other world exists. They have not had any opportunities to be exposed to it, but when we share it with them, it's pretty exciting. We use the materials we have access to through professional coaching to show our clients that they can be something different than they are today.

We belong to four different coaching programs, all with different areas of focus—retirement planning, entrepreneurship, practice management, and marketing. We also subscribe to materials from Dr. Alan Zimmerman, professional speaker and trainer, on topics such as leadership and personal development, and Darren Hardy, creator of *SUCCESS* magazine and a mentor to achievers.

We get a lot of resources from those programs. As a result, we are getting inundated with a positive can-do mentality. We spend a lot of time and effort learning from the best of the best so that we can transfer that powerfully valuable knowledge to our clients.

About the Author

Bryan Sweet, CLU®, ChFC®, MSFS, CFS
Founder and CEO, Sweet Financial Services,
Wealth Advisor, RJFS*
Creator of The Dream Architect™
Cofounder, Dare to Dream Enterprises**

Since the start of his financial services career in 1979, Bryan Sweet has specialized in helping individuals accumulate and preserve wealth for retirement and beyond. A native of Fairmont, Minnesota, Bryan earned his master's degree in financial services from The American College in Bryn Mawr, Pennsylvania, before embarking on what would become a lifelong career as a wealth management consultant.

He established his own independent firm, Sweet Financial Services, in 1987 and aligned with Raymond James in 1989. Since 2004, Bryan has been a member of the Raymond James Chairman's Council,*** which is composed of the firm's most successful financial advisors. Bryan has been recognized by multiple industry publications as one of the top financial advisors in the United States, and he has earned membership in *Research Magazine*'s Hall of Fame.**** In addition, Sweet Financial Services has been named to the *Inc.* magazine Top 5000 list of the fastest-growing private companies since 2014.*****

It is because of Bryan's passion in working with some of his best clients that he decided to develop Dare to Dream Enterprises. He has been an avid member of Strategic Coach, which has helped provide the clarity he needed in his business. He found that he works best with high-net-worth business owners who have complex financial needs. In working with these clients, helping move them toward living their retirement dreams, it became evident that all too often, people don't dream big enough. Dare to Dream Enterprises helps provide clarity in a world of chaos so that people are able to focus on the things in life that matter most to them. Dare to Dream supports business owners, women in transition, and others who are looking to build a bigger future and take control of their lives.

*Located at 1300 South Prairie Avenue, Fairmont MN 56031. Telephone: 507-235-5587. Securities offered through Raymond James Financial Services Inc., Member FINRA/SIPC.

** Dare to Dream Enterprises is not affiliated with Raymond James.

*** Membership is based on prior fiscal year production. Requalification is required annually.

**** Criteria include a minimum of 15 years in the industry, having acquired substantial assets under management, demonstration of superior client service, and having earned recognition from the company's peers and the broader community.

***** The 2016 Inc. 5000 is ranked according to percentage revenue growth when comparing 2012 to 2015. To qualify, companies must have been founded and generating revenue by March 31, 2012. They had to be US-based, privately held, for profit, and independent—not subsidiaries or divisions of other companies—as of December 31, 2015. (Since then, a number of companies on the list have gone public or been acquired.) The minimum revenue required for 2012 was $100,000; the minimum for 2015 was $2 million. As always, *Inc.* reserves the right to decline applicants for subjective reasons. Companies on the Inc. 500 are featured in *Inc.*'s September issue and at inc.com/inc5000.

About the Contributors

Oliver Kollofski
Partner and Director of Wealth Services,
Sweet Financial Services
Investment Advisor Representative, RJFS

Oliver joined Sweet Financial Services in 2007 as Director of Wealth Services. His passion lies in building creative planning strategies to help clients have the freedom to focus on what matters most to them.

Growing up, he had an interest in problem solving as well as building relationships. Wanting to merge these interests into a career, he attended the University of Northern Iowa, where he earned degrees in finance and real estate.

Today, Oliver leads the planning and investment departments at Sweet Financial Services, where he became partner in 2013. He is a CERTIFIED FINANCIAL PLANNER™ professional and a Certified Private Wealth Advisor. Oliver is also a member of Ed Slott's Elite IRA Advisor group.

Oliver lives in Fairmont with his wife, Emily, and sons, Jace and Van. Outside the office, he enjoys spending time with his family, coaching hockey, and attending youth sporting events.

Brittany Anderson
Chief Operating Officer, Sweet Financial Services
Office Manager, RJFS
Cofounder, Dare to Dream Enterprises*

Brittany Anderson joined Sweet Financial Services in 2008. Her goal is to harmonize the office so the staff is focused on providing personalized service and inspiring guidance to clients. She works closely with Bryan in the strategic planning of the firm, oversees the day-to-day operations, and provides leadership to the team in her management role.

She has been a member of Strategic Coach, which has helped her to uncover her true passion—engaging teams and motivating people to be the best version of themselves, all while taking an objective look at a firm to create processes and procedures to move it toward being a self-managed and multiplying company.

It was through this process that Brittany and Bryan decided to create Dare to Dream Enterprises, a firm that helps provide clarity in a world of chaos so that people are able to focus on the things in life that matter most to them. Dare to Dream supports business owners, women in transition, and others looking to build a bigger future and take control of their lives.

A graduate of Minnesota State University–Mankato, Brittany holds a bachelor's degree in business management.

Brittany lives in rural Sherburn, Minnesota, with her husband, David, and daughter, Jersey. In her free time, she enjoys spending quality time with her family, working on her latest repurposing project, and spending time outdoors.

---

* Dare to Dream Enterprises is not affiliated with Raymond James.

About The Marilyn Sweet-Borchardt Education Foundation

All proceeds from the sale of this book will be donated to The Marilyn Sweet-Borchardt Education Foundation. I established this foundation to help single women who have children going to college. Through the foundation, we give out grants to help the children of those single moms go to school. I established this foundation in honor of my mom, who was in a similar position and sacrificed so much to allow me to get a better education.

Currently we are able to help support two young people each year, and as the fund grows, we will expand the number of grants we provide.

Raymond James is not affiliated with The Marilyn Sweet-Borchardt Education Foundation.

Made in the USA
Charleston, SC
20 December 2016